Unacceptable Losses

How Easy Access to Firearms Encourages Massacres and Gun Violence

By Michael M. Nunes

Cover Photograph, Pulse Nightclub. By user Walter.
Creative Commons License found here:
<https://creativecommons.org/licenses/by/2.0/ >
Photo found here:
<https://www.flickr.com/photos/walterpro/28089572824/in/photostream/ >

Other Cover Photographs from <www.pixabay.com>

To all the people who have lost their lives in gun massacres,

murders, suicides, and justifiable homicide because of our

obsession with the Second Amendment rather than our respect

for human life.

Contents

Preface

I am no firearms expert, I am not an instructor, or gun owner, I do not frequent gun shows or shop for firearms, I have never read Field & Stream or any affiliated publication, and have no desire to do so. My experience with guns extends as far as the military service I was compelled to undergo as a South African citizen. During that service, I carried a fully automatic weapon, an R-1, otherwise known as an FN FAL battle rifle, which was to the best of my memory, a Belgian weapon used during the occupation of the Belgian Congo. I know how to disassemble, otherwise known as fieldstripping for inspection, and reassemble the weapon, mostly for cleaning, since that was what we did most. My particular weapon was probably one of the first ever produced; it had a wooden stock and the barrel was slightly scored, which meant that it never looked clean, and passing daily inspections was tough, despite spending hours with toothbrush and 2x4 pull-through cleaning the weapon. I fired the weapon only a few times in training, an ordeal I prefer not to repeat.

As a member of the South African Defense Force, guns surrounded me throughout my time in the service. The defense force supported the apartheid regime, invaded other nations, treated the locals with contempt, and it had contempt for the ordinary citizens, like me, who were forced to serve or spend time in jail if we chose to refuse. It was only four years after my service that I was able to fully extricate myself from the military. This was, I hoped, the last time I would ever see an assault weapon.

During the first year after my service, the prevailing gun culture and high crime rate in South Africa persuaded me to purchase a 9mm semi-automatic pistol. It jammed incessantly and the cost of shooting at paper targets became exorbitant.

I left South Africa partly because of the escalating frequency of gun violence. The military weapons left over from the guerilla war in South West Africa, now Namibia, became part of a crime wave that swept the country, sending the murder rate soaring to levels not seen anywhere on Earth outside war zones. In addition, (mostly white) South African owned the many legal guns in the country. These weapons were often used to murder their children and their wives, and to take their own lives, or were stolen during the many robberies across the country.

I hoped that the United States would prove to be safer in terms of its gun policy, given its position as the world's superpower. While South Africa had a strong gun culture, the U.S. takes gun ownership to a completely new level, a fascination that creates an unnecessarily dangerous society for us all. At first, this did not bother me much, since I was working hard and had little time to debate political or social policy. As a foreign consultant on a work contract, I did not believe that I would be here for long, so much of the debate washed over me.

As it turned out, I remained here in the United States, eventually attaining citizenship. Over time, I became aware of the various political debates raging in Washington, but the gun debate was particularly muted in comparison to other debates, especially after 9/11. After the shooting at Virginia Tech, I became more interested in the gun debate, but not enough to learn more about it. Aurora, Colorado brought the issue sharply into focus.

The single incident that riveted my attention and set me on the path to write this book was the brutal slaughter of twenty young children and their six teachers at the Sandy Hook Elementary School in Newtown, Connecticut. The access to semi-automatic weapons allowed Adam Lanza to slaughter so many people in so short a space of time. For me, that event should have awakened the American public to the harsh realities of gun violence. That it did not, that these young children and their teachers were never given justice is something that cannot pass without criticism.

I have written this book as a testament to my indignation and sorrow at the inability of Congress, the inflexibility of the gun lobby, and the inability of the American people to tackle the largely preventable and inordinately high rate of death by gun.

My personal view is that firearms ought to be strictly restricted in their ownership and their use. However, I also believe that change will only come when we acknowledge the concerns of gun owners and weigh those concerns against the steadily rising toll of death and injury. Extremism breeds extremism, and American society has become entrenched in extreme views of gun ownership or its absence. Intransigence in the gun lobby regarding lack of regulation breeds a view that opposes ownership. I believe that there is a middle ground, that there are ways to come to a consensus. We need both sides to understand that the right to life and safety from gun violence must be the primary concern of any agreements. We cannot have a society tilted in favor of the ownership of firearms without ensuring that people opposed to ownership feel safe in public spaces, schools, shopping malls or nightclubs.

It is up to members of Congress to look at the problem with integrity; allow comprehensive weapons legislation to pass through the House and Senate. To members of Congress, that have only obstructed sensible changes to the gun culture, the judgment of history will not be kind. Neither will this book.

I am well aware that the Second Amendment is highly controversial, and I have been deliberately controversial in turn. This nation needs an honest, full-throated gun debate, not one in which the people are intimidated by a small, vocal minority of gun owners. We need the facts, and I intend to provide as many as I am able. The entire nation, including the gun lobby have a moral obligation to ensure that unarmed civilians can go about their business in safety, without being concerned that their lives will be taken by armed men. Any society as armed as is the United States cannot make that assurance. It is up to Congress to make that happen.

I must acknowledge the many articles that I used in writing this book, the value of the on-line encyclopedia www.wikipedia.org in referencing many of those articles, the images I obtained from the artists at www.pixabay.com, and images licensed under the Creative Commons.

I have used a picture of a generic church and classroom on my cover. I do not in any way imply that the actual church or school was involved in any gun violence whatsoever. I intend only to show that any public venue may be the object of a massacre. I sincerely hope that no such event ever occurs in either place. The Las Vegas welcome sign similarly is only intended to show that a massacre occurred in that city, not that the entire city is at all to blame for what happened. The memorial around the Pulse Nightclub sign is placed on the page out of sympathy for the victims.

My thoughts are always with the victims, their families and the community. Only when we concentrate on the victims of gun violence can we solve this problem.

Introduction

This book looks at the Stand Your Ground laws and how it legitimized homicide, including the unjustified shooting death of Trayvon Martin.

The gun lobby presses vociferously for greater access to firearms by criminals, potential terrorists, the severely mentally ill, those with restraining orders against them, and even children. By doing nothing to alleviate gun violence, they are, together with Congress directly responsible for the slaughter of tens of thousands each year. The deaths can be reduced dramatically as they have been in other developed nations, but given the power of the gun industry and the gun lobby, this is not happening.

Members of Congress are reminiscent of rag dolls being tossed about by a voracious gun lobby mastiff rather than legislators from the self-professed greatest representative democracy in history. The fawning timidity of Congress toward the gun industry and its acolytes has all the hallmarks of a nation falling under the spell of an authoritarian organization rather than an independent, democratic superpower. Even President Obama appeared resigned to living in a nation increasingly run by conservative forces, whose solution to social disputes lies in violence, and an unwillingness to take on the gun industry.

Civilians do not need to possess firearms, especially extreme firearms. The singular purpose for which firearms are produced is to kill in a more efficient manner. They have no other functional purpose. They are killing machines whose only function is to destroy and extinguish life. A kitchen knife is intended to cut meat or vegetables; a tire iron is intended to change tires. A gun is intended only to kill and it exists for no other reason. A gun does nothing of value; it does not cure the sick, solve scientific puzzles, improve people's lives, or build anything important. Guns destroy, that is their intended purpose, and the reason gun owners want guns that kill in ever more efficient ways.

A civilized state is obliged to make it increasingly difficult for people to kill one another, by whatever method. The most effective method people have found for spontaneously killing one another is the personal firearm. Nothing is as effective at targeting specific people so efficiently and fatally. That is why we need to regulate who may own and carry these weapons.

The rights of vulnerable groups always appear to surrender before the presumptive rights of the persecutors. The state has a compelling interest in preventing violence to any resident, and thus the prevention of that violence must take precedence over the disputable right to property.

We cherish our freedom to move through society without recourse to large numbers of armed men patrolling our streets to keep us safe from armed gun owners. The most rational option is to restrict gun ownership, and remove the need for armed guards. Besides, that is what law enforcement is for, but then, the gun lobby is not notably supportive of law enforcement. They appear to prefer untrained, well-armed vigilantes roaming the streets picking fights to a society governed by laws to secure the rights of the vulnerable.

I refuse to acknowledge that the Second Amendment confers a right to possess firearms without stringent regulations and restrictions governing their use. The amendment makes abundantly clear that the intention of gun possession is service to the state, and not the tumultuous nihilism portrayed by the gun lobby.

Self Defense and Decriminalized Homicide

The Stand Your Ground law, as introduced in Florida, is an egregious instance of legislative ineptitude run amok. This cruel and inhumane law led to the extra-judicial killing of young teenager, Trayvon Martin, who was engaged in nothing more sinister than carrying iced tea and a packet of Skittles. His transgression was being in the wrong place at the wrong time, faced with an over-zealous vigilante, and gunned down. His killing deserves an entire chapter as an example of the dangerous actions of conservative legislatures.

The Needless Brutality of ALEC

The American Legislative Exchange Council (ALEC) pushed the initial Stand-Your-Ground laws, with support from the National Rifle Association (NRA). The NRA offered the original template for the law to ALEC. Marion Hammer, a representative from the NRA, assisted in drafting the bill, lobbying heavily for its passage in Florida[1]. Law enforcement officials warned that this law would make it more difficult to convict people of homicide, since defendants would simply claim self-defense, placing the burden of proof on prosecutors, and on the dead[2]. The Association of Prosecuting Attorneys says that the laws are not merely an extension of the castle doctrine, but a barrier to the prosecution of criminals.

ALEC is an industry group backed by the wealthy Koch brothers to advance legislation that they perceive is in the best interests of the business community. Legislation like the Stand-Your-Ground law is provided to right-wing legislators as a template that can be followed in a number of states.

Wal-mart, the giant discount retailer, was the head of the task force in ALEC that passed the 2005 Castle Doctrine Act. Wal-mart is also the largest seller of rifles and ammunition in the United

States. Their motive in passing these laws is not to improve the safety and security of citizens, but to increase sales of their products, regardless of citizens' safety. Much of the gun violence that we see across the United States can be laid at their door.

The ALEC/NRA bills proffer legal immunity to a person anywhere they have a right to be. Some states, such as Wisconsin, include only those areas surrounding a person's home or business and for those instances in which the occupant believes that an intruder was entering their property unlawfully. These provisions are the most controversial part of these laws, since they expand the number of areas that apply to the laws to any place that a person has a legal right to be.

Following the death of Trayvon Martin at the hands of George Zimmerman, a number of large companies terminated their relationship with ALEC, not because of the immorality of the laws introduced by ALEC, but due to adverse media publicity. These companies voluntarily associated with a group that promoted laws legitimizing murder. ALEC subsequently announced that it would get rid of its task force on non-economic issues[3], which was done under pressure from groups like Common Cause. However, it continues to push ahead on issues, like Stand Your Ground laws, that disproportionately target poorer communities and the poor wage earner. Groups belonging to ALEC included companies like Coca Cola, Wal-Mart, AT&T, McDonalds and the Bill and Melinda Gates Foundation, all of whom must share blame in the drafting of these laws.

Stand Your Ground The Most Dangerous Law

In 2005, Florida introduced its Stand Your Ground law, which expanded the list of places in which a person does not have to retreat and may stand his ground. This law also prevents the victim or the victim's family from initiating civil litigation against the killer, thus removing the threat of legal liability. The law states that a person is presumed to have a reasonable fear of imminent peril of death or bodily injury to himself or another when using defensive force that is intended to cause death or bodily injury to another. These new laws eliminate the obligation to retreat where possible, and create an entirely new set of dangers to people in public places.

The Stand Your Ground law reads in part,

"The right to stand his or her ground and meet force with force, including deadly force if he or she reasonably believes it is necessary to do so, to prevent death or great bodily harm to himself or herself or another."

The wording of this law is such that any altercation in which deadly force is used can be excused by invoking the reasonable belief of great bodily harm or death. Since no judge or jury can determine what a person might be thinking during an altercation, they have no alternative other than to accept the invocation of this law. The definition of *"great bodily harm"* is so nebulous as to be worthless. One person may have an entirely different view of what this phrase means. It is feasible that a great many homicides might fall within the parameters of this law, allowing killers to remain on the streets.

Jeb Bush, Governor of Florida supported the measure because; *"to have to retreat and put yourself in a very precarious position defies common sense"*[4]. The laws preclude the need to retreat, which itself defies common sense. If a person is in the position to retreat, they should be legally obligated to do so, to minimize harm to others. It is common sense not to take lethal action unless it is absolutely imperative and unavoidable.

John F. Timoney, Miami's police chief called the bill dangerous and unnecessary. The chief, who has pushed his own officers to use less deadly force, said that many more people including children could become victims. People, including those "with road rage, or drunken sports fans, could believe they have immunity from prosecution"[5]. In the years following passage, children have indeed been killed using these laws as legal cover for lethal acts. The chief also said that, *you are encouraging people to use deadly force where it shouldn't be used*.

Other police chiefs including Chuck Harmon of the St. Petersburg police, and Sheriff Ken Jeffe of Broward County also opposed the bill. As the departments that have to deal with incidents of gun death, these people are in the best position to decide whether these laws are needed.

Between the years 2000 and 2010, at least 20 states introduced stand-your ground laws, enhancing self-defense laws otherwise known as the "Castle Doctrine". Before the introduction of these laws, the common law standards for self-defense included the right to defend ones home, or "Castle" from intruders. The Stand Your Ground laws are also known as "Shoot First" laws, that alter the centuries old "Castle Doctrine" that allows people the right of self-defense in their homes. The right to defend ones home without retreat is well established historically and did not need any modification.

Governor Scott Walker, of Wisconsin, signed a 2011 bill into law called the "Castle Doctrine Act". This bill resembled a bill drawn up by ALEC and the NRA. The bill allowed the killer of a young man who hid on a porch after police broke up an underage drinking party, to be released without charge. The homeowner shot the 20 year old, a young black male, who was unarmed at the time of the incident. It strains credibility to believe that the homeowner was in clear and present danger from someone outside his home. At the very most, the young man was guilty of trespass, a misdemeanor for which there are legal remedies that do not include arbitrary execution.

A loose reading of the laws may lead many to believe that there is no burden of proof on the killer to show that his life was in imminent danger. A killer that claims Stand-Your-Ground is taken at his word unless there are sufficient credible witnesses to the crime. In most developed countries, the killer is charged with a crime, albeit justifiable homicide, and he must show just cause for his actions. In other words, his life must demonstrably be in danger before he is able to take lethal action. With Stand Your Ground laws, the killer does not have to demonstrate that his life was indeed in imminent danger or that anything less than lethal force was necessary to prevent harm to his person. The onus is placed on the deceased to show that he was not a lethal threat.

Florida enacted the law with support from the Republican-controlled house and senate. The National Rifle Association led lobbying for the law, stating that they required immunity for gunmen who might use deadly force against unarmed individuals imagined to be threatening[6]. This despite being warned that innocent people like Trayvon Martin might be killed unnecessarily by people invoking the law. The Martin family supports a Trayvon amendment that would make it harder for someone who starts a fight to use the self-defense argument under the law[7].

The number of concealed weapon permits issued in Florida has jumped significantly, from 347,000 to 979,000. That is, one in nineteen people you meet in Florida is likely to carry a concealed weapon. However, given that of the nineteen million people in Florida, four million are children[8], one in every fifteen people you meet is likely to have a concealed weapons permit. Since men are three times more likely to own a firearm than are women, at least one in every ten men you meet is likely to be armed. Thus, an increasing number of people carry guns in public due to these laws, and are prepared to use them. This increases the chance of accidental shootings, or shooting motivated by heightened emotion during altercations.

A History of Reasonable Self-Defense

U.S. self defense laws derive primarily from English Common Law, which provides that a person has a duty to retreat before using deadly force against an assailant, as long as that retreat can be done in safety. The exception is that a person threatened in ones home may use deadly force to stop an assault[9].

Self-defense inasmuch as it relates to the protection of a person, members of his family, or property is a universally accepted right, despite what the NRA and other gun advocates believe about the United Nations. They perpetrate the erroneous belief that the U.N. would abrogate the right to self-defense. The Universal Declaration of Human Rights says this about self-defense[10],

> "No one shall be subject to arbitrary interference with his privacy, family, home or correspondence, nor to attacks upon his honor and reputation. Everyone has the right to the protection of the law against such interference or attacks."

In practice, this means that, "given the states monopoly of force, those authorized by the state to defend the law are charged with the use of necessary force to protect such rights"[11]. In the absence of such deterrent, a person has the right to defend himself, his family and property, within certain constraints. A person has an ethical obligation to ensure that he uses the minimum force necessary to repel an attack, the operative term here being "minimum force necessary". The Stand Your Ground laws extend the right to use unnecessary lethal force during events for which it is not warranted, which alters precedent from the minimum to the maximum force necessary to prevent an attack.

If a person is able to retreat from a situation safely, without jeopardizing his own life, he has an ethical obligation to do so. The use of force cannot include the use of deadly force in the absence of a compelling reason to use it. A person's life must be shown to be in danger, with no reasonable possibility of retreat before deadly force can be used justifiably. Any use of force to dispel an attack that exceeds this boundary amounts to self-defense using excessive force, and ought to be prosecuted as a standard case of homicide or manslaughter.

Under civil law, most sensible legal systems use the theory of "abuse of right" to justify the denial of the self defense mechanism when fighting off an attack. In English common law the approach is as follows[12],

> "A defendant is entitled to use reasonable force to protect himself, others for
> whom he is responsible and his property. It must be reasonable."

The operative term in this sentence is "reasonable", and this is where America's Stand Your Ground laws abandon the bounds of civilized society and a thousand years of common law tradition. By allowing individuals to carry the "Castle Doctrine" with them wherever they go, the use of deadly force formerly reserved for the state now extends to the individual. It is this principle that succeeds in making American society a far more dangerous and anarchic place than it has ever been. The obsession with a single individual right over the diverse rights of society or communities creates an individualized "state" empowered to carry out death sentences against not just actual felonious activity, but perceived or imagined felonious activity.

The concept of the Castle Doctrine is clearly intended to allow property owners to protect that property from unlawful entry. By expanding this doctrine to any place a person has a right to be, the concept of the Castle becomes redundant. By definition, a public place is no single persons private domain, and everyone has as much right to be in that place as anyone else, so the Castle Doctrine ought not to be valid.

How the State Fails In Its Obligation to Defend the Individual

We as a nation are returning to a time when armed predators prey on unarmed civilians, where those with arms pick fights in order to kill innocent civilians, or any civilians who have no armed force of their own. This is a Wild West scenario, with the fastest draw, or most powerful weapon being the winner, and people die without recourse or security under the law. It creates a lawless society in which the strong prey on the weak and the justice system rules for the strong. Gun owners now constitute a major threat to a safe, secure and peaceful society.

The first duty of a state or nation is abundantly clear. It must protect and defend the integrity of the state, and ensure the safety and security of all its citizens, not just those that bear arms. Those people residing within the state have a right to be safe from terror, from fear of death at the hands of armed gun owners, whether they own a weapon or not. The Stand Your Ground laws have stripped that right from their citizens and extended the right only to those prepared to bear arms. The state has thus failed in its fundamental duty to all people living within its borders.

Immunity from Prosecution or Investigation

These laws now impute credibility to the belief of the perpetrator that there was an imminent threat of death or bodily harm, whether or not there was any credence to that belief. Anyone that now makes that claim is immune from prosecution or civil liability. That violates the victims' civil liberties, since he is no longer in a position to dispute the claim.

In addition, the law continues to state that the finder of fact, or the investigator, may not consider whether the killer had the opportunity to flee or retreat before he used deadly force. The reasonable expectation that the least amount of force necessary to contain a situation must be considered before taking action now appears anachronistic. Lethal force has become the first course of action, rather than the last and most extreme.

Since law enforcement does not keep records concerning their decisions when deciding not to press charges in a Stand-Your-Ground case, it is not feasible to produce an analysis of these decisions. There are no records that determine how many of these motions have been filed, or of their outcomes. An ever-increasing number of people are using these laws to justify extreme violence and force, to deal with everyday occurrences that have never before justified force.

Vigilantism Replaces Law Enforcement

Stand Your Ground laws allow ordinary citizens, without adequate training, to use lethal force, without a full appreciation of the law, or of the moral or ethical implications of their actions. It is difficult enough for trained law enforcement officers to perform according to established protocols in a deadly situation, and almost impossible for untrained gun owners to act appropriately. The unprotected population is now at the mercy of people who often have scant understanding or appreciation of the law and who mete out justice on an entirely arbitrary basis.

The Tyranny of Self-Defense

The right to self-defense in any public setting now belongs to those who possess the greater force, or those who carry firearms. Those who do not, have lost their right to self-defense because of the greater force possessed by the gun owner. In any altercation, whether it is violent or not, a persons' life can be forfeited if he does not carry a firearm for protection. In a peaceful society, an individual knows how rules are interpreted and when his life is in jeopardy. People are now encouraged to solve their differences with firearms rather than through the courts.

A simple misunderstanding of the boundaries of self-defense laws like Stand Your Ground might lead to death. We live with the fear of death in what has become an anarchic society. The entire intent of the laws, that no one has the obligation to retreat, is now dominated by whoever possesses the greater force.

Outside the bounds of Western Civilization, self-defense applies far more loosely, often without restrictions on the use of reasonable or proportionate force based on the severity of the crime. This is where American jurisprudence is headed, towards Third World nihilism and contempt for the state. The difference is that in the United States, a crime is not necessary for the use of disproportionate force, only the perception that a violent crime might be committed unless force is applied.

Rep. Dennis Baxley says that the statute itself does not discriminate based on race or gender and that a study might bring to light how it is currently applied. It is not because of race or gender that the statute discriminates, it discriminates between those that are armed, and those that are not. Clearly, an armed individual has the use of greater force than does someone who is unarmed. Even aggravated assault is ultimately preferable to death. The overarching principle should always be, first do no harm, and if possible, do the least amount of harm possible to prevent a threat. These laws thus give a greater right to self-defense to those that are armed, as opposed to those that have only their physical attributes with which to protect themselves. In this case, the law sides with the greater threat and places the unarmed victim at a great disadvantage.

Once a person is dead, the killer cannot prove that the victim was intending to kill him, or even do him great bodily harm. If an angry individual confronts someone, he cannot claim that the person was planning to harm him in any way, without a physical attack. A perceived threat does not necessarily translate into an actual threat. We should not be able to take a life if someone attacks us without the intention of killing us. It is up to the judicial system to ensure justice, not up to armed belligerents.

Stand Your Ground laws give all the power in any situation to those that are armed, and prejudice those who are not. A corpse tells no tales, especially if the gun owner is given the benefit of the doubt without any investigation by law enforcement. These laws essentially force the population to arm itself in order to at least level the playing field, which is the intent of the laws. The intention was never to make society safer; it was always to increase profits for the gun industry and their lobbying arm, the National Rifle Association.

The Cheapening of Life

The legal *volteface* that has gripped the United States since the introduction of the Stand Your Ground laws is of grave concern. Before these laws, the U.S. was moving to the philosophical understanding that life is precious, and that we should extend greater civil liberties to all people. With the introduction of the

Stand Your Ground laws, life has become a lot cheaper; the taking of a life without prosecution carries a lesser penalty than any misdemeanor. A misdemeanant now receives a greater penalty for spitting on the sidewalk than he does for the killing of a human being. This cheapens life, which is now worth little more than the cost of a bullet.

These laws have resulted in an atmosphere of fear of the people around us. It makes us all less safe if everyone is armed and legally able to take a life. We should not have to spend our lives worrying about whether the next altercation we have will lead to our deaths. People do argue, that is part of life. It should not mean the end of that life.

In the last resort killing of another human being, a person should at least have the duty to show just cause, to show that his actions were not premeditated and that he had no recourse other than the taking of a life. The victim ought to have the right to have the case heard before a jury and the evidence brought to light. With these laws we are taking the word of the killer that his actions were justified, opening the door to legitimized, state sanctioned murder, or summary execution for few or no legal infractions.

The Presumption of Fear and Civil Liability

It is troubling that at least eight states do not include a presumption of reasonable fear in their Stand Your Ground laws. This means that lethal force can be used in circumstances in which an individual merely believes that he is being forced to retreat, without an accompanying threat to life or of bodily injury.

What is worse, 18 states have removed the right to civil liability. Anyone who believes that he has been wronged thus has no redress of grievances under the law, and nor do his relatives. There are often no investigations carried out at all. Even law enforcement officers do not investigate the crime scene to determine whether a crime has been perpetrated or not.

It is perverse that if you push someone intentionally, you can be charged with assault; if you discharge a firearm into the ceiling while being threatened, you can receive twenty years, as happened with Marissa Alexander when confronted by her abusive husband[13]. Yet, you could kill someone with a firearm, claim Stand Your Ground, and be released without investigation or charge. We have perverted our justice system to the degree that homicide receives no sentence, but simple assault can end with a lengthy prison sentence.

Exemption and Immunity from Liability

From a legal perspective, the Stand Your Ground law reduces the legal and social cost to the claimant of killing a person. Since there is no criminal liability, or civil litigation route for the victim's family, the claimant may take a life with the reasonable expectation that there will be no expensive legal defense of his actions. This removes an obstacle from the path of a claimant, who is now more likely to use lethal force, secure in the knowledge that neither the law, nor the family can punish him.

These laws also eliminate the expectation that the claimant will face criminal liability, and its associated legal costs. Once society lowers the bar, invocation of the law in any murder is likely to increase, with a greater number of potential defenders receiving no punishment for their crime. Thus, lowering the threshold for the justified use of force produces more of it[14].

Proponents claim that these laws extend additional immunity from civil and criminal liability to citizens that are otherwise law-abiding. The inference is that the decision to use lethal force is taken in a short space of time; therefore the claimant should be given more leeway than in other cases. In reality, a claimant is more likely to use this defense in a moment of surging emotion, rather than ponder the ramifications of his action. The pressure is to act immediately without the threat of civil or criminal action.

In most developed nations, the burden of proof in the case of self-defense is on the claimant, rather than on the victim. Since, in the case of lethal force used during Stand Your Ground, the victim is no longer around to defend himself, the claimant is free to act, secure in the knowledge that the victim has no defense. The presumption of a reasonable fear of imminent death or injury places a burden of proof not on the perpetrator, but on the prosecutor to show otherwise[15].

These laws introduce the concept of a presumption of immunity for a killer who claims that he was acting in self-defense. Instead of asserting self-defense before a jury, these laws grant legal immunity to people who invoke the laws. Normal self-defense laws provide a defense against prosecution, whereas these new laws provide immunity from prosecution. In many cases, people are immune even from arrest or from investigation into the causes of the killing.

Under these laws, anyone invoking the law is extended the presumption of reasonable fear for his life, or even just an unlawful threat and thus the use of lethal force against a presumed assailant, without an obligation to retreat. The Stand-Your-Ground laws expand the self-defense concept to any area outside the home, permitting the use of lethal force in self-defense. This includes defense of a vehicle, but it may apply to all lawfully occupied locations.

If there are no criminal or civil sanctions against him, he is far more likely to take the option of lethal force. Immunity from prosecution creates a greater propensity for violence. In normal self-defense law, a person must understand that he is likely to have to explain his actions before a judge or a jury.

These laws also produce a lack of confidence in the ability of the judicial system to provide justice for injury or death produced by these laws. This should lead to mistrust in the systems' ability to protect victims of Stand-Your-Ground laws, mistrust in authority, and ultimately a mistrust of others in society. If one believes that they are unsafe in any public place, it creates suspicion and fear in the population, and societal schism.

Not a Polite Society, But One Filled with Fear

Some proponents have offered as a defense of such laws that they produce a society that is more polite and civil. They misconstrue the underlying social pathology. People become more fearful of one another, and afraid that any action can cause offense that may result in lethal action.

I remember shouting at a truck that went through a pedestrian crossing outside a local supermarket. Now, perhaps I was a little hasty, but considering that there are many pedestrians walking around, the driver ought to have been more careful. The driver screamed to a stop, whipped open the door and started shouting and swearing angrily.

I walked away quietly, since it suddenly struck me that he might be armed, and my own life could end swiftly. Fortunately, the incident went no further. My own right to stand my ground had just been destroyed by fear. Since I was not armed, I had to retreat in ignominy before this verbal onslaught. If I had been, I could justifiably have stood my ground and used a weapon with complete immunity. Since I was not, the incident ended, as it should, without harm to either party, other than a bruised ego.

It remains with me that if the individual in this incident had decided to pull a weapon, I would have had absolutely no recourse at all. I could well have been seen as the instigator, and thus deserving of a death sentence. From the cases that I have seen, even running away is no defense against these laws. A person can be legitimately executed, and the perpetrator granted immunity.

People must be able to argue, even vehemently, in favor of a given point of view without having to face arbitrary death when perceived as a threat. Not all perceived threats are necessarily life threatening, even when delivered with anger. It is a violation of ones right to free speech to be killed for expressing an emotion. Only once that expression of emotion becomes a tangible physical threat can force be used. Otherwise, it is mere posturing. Many people are paranoid, and see other people and events as potential threats. These laws allow them to act out their paranoid fantasies with impunity, free from prosecution.

These laws are used to prevent death, bodily harm, or any forcible felony based only on a person's perception of the victim. The justice system asks only three questions; did the assailant have the right to be in that place? Was he engaged in a lawful activity? Did he have a reasonable fear of death or great bodily harm? Victims must now determine what and how other people are thinking in order to prevent being killed for some petty reason.

Any social situation could have the potential for being seen as a physical threat. Members of the public must now weigh any social situation carefully, lest it be seen as constituting a threat to someone. A loud word, a look, bumping into someone, or mistakes while driving may be seen as threatening and result in death. This allows anyone to pick a fight, kill someone who retaliates and claim his Stand-Your-Ground rights.

The benefit of the doubt under these laws is always with the killer, not the victim, turning centuries of legal precedent on its head and making for frightening social interactions and implications. Without any evidence to the contrary, the protections of these laws prevail in court. Conservative laws have overturned ancient precedent penalizing murder and replaced them with laws legitimizing and justifying murder.

Why Firearm Owners Have a Greater Right to Stand Their Ground

An armed person has a greater right to occupy any location than does the unarmed person. The armed individual has now taken from others their right to be anywhere unhindered. In any altercation, all participants have an equal right to stand their ground. By using lethal force, the armed person has stripped all other occupants of their right to be in that place. It is difficult for anyone who is not armed to argue that they are standing their ground and have as much right to be in that place as those that are armed.

Civilians are making life or death decisions about other people, acting as judge, jury and executioner, in which victims have no legal rights. These civilians are not trained, nor are they obligated to obtain training in the legal, moral and ethical implications of killing another human being. Their impulsive actions and lack of training cause fatalities, and society has no way to exact punishment or protect itself. There is no civic power to which they are accountable for their actions.

A person carrying a concealed weapon has a significant advantage over a person not similarly armed. In an altercation, it is to the advantage of the armed person to use lethal force and claim Stand-Your-Ground regardless of whether his life was in danger.

An unarmed victim thus relinquishes his right and ability to claim Stand-Your-Ground because his opponent is armed.

In any social interaction in which an altercation is involved, an unarmed person who does not intend to harm others cannot know how much emotion or anger to show anyone. Any display of anger could be seen as a threat to another person, justifying the use of lethal force. The average person's right to show disapproval of anti-social behavior is severely curtailed by these laws. People cannot know what is in the mind of others, or what is likely to represent a threat to others.

Another criticism of these laws is that they favor the rights of those invoking Stand-Your-Ground over those of victims of the laws, who receive no justice. It takes us back to a time when women were accused of being the initiators of rape rather than its victim. With these laws, the gun owner is extended greater rights than a victim without a weapon.

Morally Ambiguous Laws

A major factor in determining whether a law is legally valid or not, is how clear the law is in defining requirements and prohibitions. If there is ambiguity in the law, or the law is unclear in any way, it ought to be struck down. The Stand Your Ground laws are increasingly shown to be vague and unclear, leaving judges and law enforcement uncertain as to the legal or moral course of action to take. Many claimants are not being prosecuted because of the uncertain nature of the laws.

The elements of a statute must be stated explicitly, with no room for ambiguity. This ensures that courts, law enforcement and individual citizens clearly understand the law and its boundaries. With Stand Your Ground laws, citizens may commit what should be criminal acts, and walk free without prosecution. Courts must evaluate laws from the standpoint of a person of ordinary intelligence who might be subject to its terms in order to determine whether it is sufficiently certain and plain[16].

The Consequences of Stand-Your-Ground

American states allow anyone believing his own life to be in danger, even if not imminent, or a subjective perception, to use deadly force against an opponent. The widening net of situations in which a person can claim to believe his life might be in danger now encompasses almost every conceivable social conflict situation. A raised voice, an angry look, a waving hand, a threatening posture can all be taken as presenting a compelling threat to an individual and used as a pretext to commit what in any civilized nation would be considered murder, or at the very least, manslaughter.

Whereas with justifiable homicide, one must present objective evidence, beyond reasonable doubt, that an intruder was intent on committing violence or a felonious act, with Stand Your Ground, a subjective claim of fear is sufficient to invoke the Castle Doctrine[17].

The French penal code states,

> "Excessive force is punishable due to disproportion between the means of defense used and the gravity of the attack defended against."

It is essential to the basic respect for human life, that society recognizes the limits of self-defense. In much of the United States, it is no longer recognized as such. Law enforcement, the judicial system and the citizens in many states are no longer clear about what is allowed and what is not. This translates to a greater number of homicides classed as justifiable, and for which the victim gets no justice. The use of disproportionate force in self-defense is now entrenched in the laws of many American states, particularly those who have introduced Stand Your Ground laws.

The Benefits and Detriments of Stand-Your-Ground Laws

There is no net benefit to society resulting from these laws. The net effect on society has been detrimental, in which more people are dying rather than fewer. Thus, these laws are a danger to an open society free from the fear of armed vigilantes.

We ought to be creating a society in which the victims of crimes are extended greater benefits, rather than expecting victims to police society. It is the place of law enforcement agencies to enforce the laws and protect society. It is the responsibility of legislators to enact laws designed to protect those most vulnerable to criminal activity. Individuals should not be expected to provide their own law enforcement, and create a culture of vigilantism.

Stand-Your-Ground laws have created a society in which there is an increase in vigilantism, and gun-owners believe that they can act with impunity against any perceived threat, whether that threat is extant or imagined. Gun-owners now look for opportunities to invoke these laws, rather than merely defending their homes from threat.

The threat to the general population at large now increases, since any altercation can result in lethal force being used against unarmed civilians. An argument over a parking space or some other trivial dispute can ultimately result in a death, against which judges are reluctant to rule.

It could be argued that any person walking down a road, who believes that someone walking towards them looks threatening, and therefore poses a threat to their life, could justifiably use lethal force. Florida State Senator Steve Geller made a similar argument[18]. Potentially, any situation that we find in everyday life could be called threatening and thus justify the use of extreme force.

Criminal Reaction To Stand Your Ground Laws

There is also the danger that the response from criminals to these laws may be to escalate violence during cases of robbery or assault, since the perceived threat from intended victims has increased. In order for the criminal to succeed in his intended course of action, he must neutralize any threat from the victim. This increases the chances that the assailant will kill a victim in the event of a robbery or assault due to the perceived hidden threat. Again, rather than making society safer, people are now less secure because of the expectation that they are armed and that lethal force will be used in retaliation against an attack.

Criminals are also more likely to ensure that they are sufficiently armed to deal with any threat from their victims, and will be more likely to use their weapons to prevent any defense mounted by the victim. Criminals who would not normally have used a weapon are now forced to arm themselves to contend with the potential threat from their targets, who are now more likely to use lethal force in an attack.

This has the effect of increasing the level of violence in society, rather than decreasing it. This makes society a far more dangerous place to live in rather than one made safer by increased firearm availability. People who are ready to take a life should have to weigh the costs of taking that life against the prospect of harm to his own life.

The Tampa Bay Times analyzed Stand Your Ground cases and found that 60% of those claiming self defense had been arrested at least once before killing someone; 30% had been accused of violent crime including assault, battery or robbery; dozens had drug arrests, 40% had three arrests or more. To date in Florida, 119 people have killed and invoked the law; those people have been arrested 327 times for property crime, violence, drugs, weapons or probation violations[19]. Thus, Stand Your Ground laws are enabling criminals and violent people to commit murder and justify it using self-defense laws.

Combating Crime or New Black Laws

These laws were not introduced to combat a wave of crime in states like Florida. Crime rates were dropping before the introduction of these laws and did not need additional legislative action. The passage of these laws were therefore not in response to increasing crime rates, and must have some other motive.

Those most at risk from these laws are invariably people of color. It is easy for those motivated by fear or prejudice to engage in vigilantism without any legal liability. US attorney Kendall Coffey described these laws as a "license to kill". It is easy to speculate that these laws were introduced to be used against people of color as a proxy for the infamous lynchings of the early twentieth century. This kind of judicial imprudence pervades societies with substantial oppressed minorities.

Proponents of these laws claim that the laws reduce crime, thus having a deterrent effect on prospective criminal activity. Evidence indicates that these laws do little to prevent robbery, larceny or aggravated assault, while leading to an increase of between eight and ten percent in murders and non-negligent manslaughter. This translates into around 600 additional homicides each year. There appears to be no detectable deterrent effect on such crimes as vehicle theft. This demonstrates that additional self-defense laws do nothing tangible to reduce the rate of crime. No evidence was found of a deterrent effect on burglary, robbery or aggravated assault[20].

Those in favor of such laws also argue that the laws have been successful in protecting people against assailants and intrusions.

We have not seen much evidence of this nature presented to us, and what is presented is dubious at best. To claim that George Zimmerman, the killer of Trayvon Martin, was justified in what he did is to stretch the boundaries of plausibility.

Zimmerman was quite capable of walking away from the incident before it became lethal, which he did not do, despite advice from law enforcement. For any incident presented, we need to determine whether there was a reasonable opportunity for the perpetrator to retreat from the incident without harm.

Another argument extended in favor of these laws is the idea that public safety was compromised after 9/11 and people wanted a greater degree of security in their lives. Frankly, a personal weapon can do nothing against a plane flying at 400mph. Nor is there much that can be done with a weapon against an IED or other explosive device, nerve gas, or poison.

People also bring up incidents like Hurricane Katrina, but there were no more deaths from gunfire during that incident than at any other time. During Hurricane Sandy, in New Jersey, there were almost no such incidents. The entire course of Hurricane Sandy was handled adequately using local police and National Guard units to maintain law and order.

The states that have introduced these laws are all states with a high black population, most likely to have a Republican governor, higher incarceration rates and a greater number of police officers. They are also more urbanized and have higher rates of poverty[21].

The Impact on Crime

If similar districts are compared, there is no change in the crime rates between those jurisdictions having extended self-defense laws and those having standard self-defense laws. The only change is that the number of justifiable homicides and other lethal force incidents that are not punished rises significantly.

A recent analysis[22] on the effect of Stand Your Ground laws on firearm related homicide attempted to determine whether Stand-Your-Ground laws made the nation any safer. Their determination was that the laws do not work in the way they were intended, they only resulted in an increase in homicides.

States are passing these laws without producing any evidence suggesting that the laws will produce a decrease in crime. The study indicates that among the white population, homicides are now increasing, particularly among white males. The study found that between 4.4 and 7.4 additional white males are killed each month, while having little or no effect on homicides in the black population.

Homicides by white men increased by an average of 7.1 percent in the states adopting Stand Your Ground laws. Additionally, hospitalizations of white males increased by 20 percent following introduction of Stand-Your-Ground along with a 60 percent increase in black females from injuries related to firearms[23]. The authors of the study hypothesize that a greater number of people may carry firearms in public and are willing to use them because of these laws. This produces an increased likelihood of guns present during self-defense incidents, leading to a rise in homicides.

In Florida, the rate of homicide was decreasing before the introduction of the Stand-Your-Ground law. After passage of the law, the homicide rate increased by 11.6 percent, according to statistics by the FDLE (Florida Department of Law Enforcement). In civilian on civilian shootings, cases rose from eight in 2004 to 57 in 2011. Between 2001 and 2005, there were an average 13.2 justifiable homicide claims in Florida, whereas there were an average 42 cases between 2006 and 2012, with a record 66 in 2012[24]. Stand Your Ground has been invoked in 93 cases with 65 deaths in Florida[25]. The laws have been invoked in bar brawls, neighbor arguments, road rage incidents and gang shootings.

According to Miami's chief of police, John Timoney[26],

"Whether its trick-or-treaters or kids playing in the yard of someone who doesn't want them there or some drunk guy stumbling into the wrong house you're encouraging people to possibly use deadly physical force where it shouldn't be used."

Griffith of the Miami-Dade State Attorneys Office had this to say[27],

"The limitations imposed on us by the Stand Your Ground laws made it impossible for any prosecutor to pursue murder charges."

In Florida, an analysis by the Palm Beach Post showed that of the cases of justifiable homicide that they looked at, the deceased were all male and unarmed, while their killers were all male and armed[28]. In all, 21 homicides were reported in which no charges were filed against the killer.

Florida has experienced a reduction in rates of robbery and aggravated assault of around 27 percent during this period. However, without figures comparing this decrease to other states, it is premature to judge whether it is due to the introduction of Stand-Your-Ground. The gun lobby has used these figures to justify their contention that these are good laws and allow people who choose to defend themselves from having to retreat in the face of threats.

Total justifiable homicides in Florida, which includes law enforcement, rose from an average 34 in 2000 to 105 in 2009. In an investigation by the Tampa Bay Times, of 200 cases in which these laws were invoked, 70 percent of perpetrators were released[29].

Their report also indicates that the laws encourage aggression in cases in which retreat was possible.

There are many reasons that the crime rate may have changed in Florida. Violent crime has been dropping nationally without the introduction of these laws. In addition, the population in Florida is aging; longer sentences are being handed out to criminal offenders; policing standards have improved, and the number of drug offenders is in decline. I cover the decline in violent crimes in a later section on the pro-gun arguments.

Before the introduction of these laws, States that adopted Stand-Your-Ground laws showed a similar trajectory in rates of homicides to states that do not adopt. After introduction, the adopting states show a statistically significant increase in the rate of homicides compared to non-adopters.

Opponents of this study propose that more deaths are being categorized as justifiable homicide, and this accounts for the discrepancy in the figures. If this were true, the total number of homicides would remain constant. This is not the case, as total homicides increase after introduction of these laws. Justifiable homicides rose by 47 percent with a 23 percent increase in non-justifiable homicides.

The result of Stand Your Ground laws has not been a decrease in crime; rather it has resulted in an increase in cases of justifiable homicide. The net result on society is that murder has now become legitimized, and claimants can perpetrate acts of violence without paying the usual penalties expected in developed countries.

The killer could also invoke these laws in situations in which there is no immediate danger other than that claimed. This leads to a wild-west culture in which citizens arm themselves in far greater numbers. Rather than provide legal cover for citizens who truly are protecting themselves, these laws encourage those involved in any altercation to use lethal force whether it is warranted or not, rather than resorting to legal remedies to resolve disputes.

This precipitates an anarchic vigilantism in which even the smallest slight or insult is interpreted as an excuse to use lethal force. Society now becomes a far more dangerous and unpredictable place in which to live, a place of fear rather than security. Rather than ensure liberty, which is claimed by those that want no laws impeding their right to own armaments, these laws restrict the personal freedoms of much of society.

Justifying Criminal Acts

These laws have also been used to justify other incidents of criminal behavior. In one instance, Kevin Michael Doerr shot and killed a black bear that wandered onto his property. The black bear is a protected species, but the man invoked the Stand-Your-Ground law, despite the fact that the bear was not aggressive, and posed no threat. The judge did not accept the plea, and Doerr was charged with a third degree felony. The bear is just as dead, regardless of the inadequate sentence.

Plaintiffs are likely to find an ever-increasing number of ways to justify criminal activity by invoking the Stand-Your-Ground laws, some in no way related to personal threats. The laws are badly written, poorly implemented and create a danger to law-abiding citizens who do not carry weapons. It marginalizes those who are not armed and takes away their right to self-defense against an opponent possessing superior armaments.

People engaged in illegal activities are also more likely to be able to invoke these laws if using lethal force. Many gangland killings could potentially be justified using these laws, and already have been. In a shoot-out between gangs, killers could well claim immunity, since they could justifiably claim that their lives were in danger. This legitimizes gang activity, and encourages it, since any participant could potentially claim self-defense.

Unequal Treatment of Perpetrators

Another problem with the enforcement of these laws is that some defendants go free after claiming Stand-Your-Ground, while others do not. Depending on who is investigating, prosecuting or adjudicating a case, the claim may be accepted or rejected. Some defendants end up in jail, and others walk free. It appears to depend entirely on the interpretation of the laws by judges or prosecutors. Many judges are uncertain of the implications or interpretation of the laws, and are often uncertain of which way to rule. This results in arbitrary application of the statutes and unfair outcomes for defendants, or for the victims of these crimes.

Since judges and prosecutors are not certain about how to rule in cases involving these laws, defendants or those that either claim immunity from the law, or are expected to make life and death decisions about whether to confront someone cannot know how assailants might act. Poorly written laws like this, that deal with life decisions, only place more peoples lives in jeopardy. A person, especially an unarmed person, should not have to make a split second decision based on a poorly written law that may cost him his life. People need to have certainty about what constitutes a threat to the life or person of another.

In one instance, Jose Ramirez was walking angrily up the driveway of his girlfriends' home, swinging his fists and flexing his muscles. The father, Owen Eugene Whitlock, killed the youth with a single shot. He was not charged. In a similar incident, Terry Tyrone Davis shot and killed his cousin as he walked up the driveway of his home with a group of friends. He will spend 25 years in jail[30].

In two other related cases, Christopher Cote hammered on his neighbors' door following an argument over Cote's dog. Jose Tapanes opened his door and shot Cote twice with a shotgun. Prosecutors rejected the killers' claim, but a jury released him. In a similar incident, Rhonda Eubanks opened her door and shot a man causing a commotion in her neighborhood. He had tried to enter her home and failed. Eubanks shot him from her doorway. She was not charged.

Innocent Bystanders

Innocent bystanders may also become victims, since during a shoot-out between armed gun owners, civilians not involved may be killed or injured. The killer can similarly claim immunity from prosecution, since he was involved in a Stand Your Ground incident. There is less motivation for a gun owner to take care that bystanders are not harmed during a shootout. Similarly, public safety personnel, or law enforcement officers could be at risk during these incidents.

A disturbing side effect of these laws is an increase in the number of bystanders, including children, being killed during shoot-outs between armed combatants. The killers are then invoking Stand Your Ground laws and are evading prosecution. Additionally, those killed are not assailants, and pose no threat to the assailant.

Retaliation from Friends and Family

There is also the issue of retaliation from the victims' families or friends. If these laws can be invoked on one side, they can potentially be invoked on the other. This could well lead to an escalation of violence and retribution, as commonly portrayed in the Sicilian Cosa Nostra. If people no longer feel that the judicial system dispenses justice or extends rights and security to them, they will increasingly take the law into their own hands, ultimately leading to a break down in civil society.

Murderers Given Their Freedom

The Tampa Bay Times analysis of Stand Your Ground also indicates that drug dealers have avoided murder charges, and allowed gang members to walk free. According to the article, there is also some evidence that the outcome of cases in which the laws are invoked can have different outcomes depending on who you are, where your case is decided and whom you kill.

Tavarious China Smith, a minor drug dealer has committed homicide on two separate occasions, two years apart, and has escaped without charge. On each occasion he invoked the "Stand Your Ground" law and was released by law enforcement. Despite the fact that he was prohibited from carrying a weapon because of prior drug convictions, he carried a Ruger .357 Magnum that he used to kill Breon Mitchell outside a nightclub[31]. Stand Your Ground laws thus allow for the arming of felons and other violent people, who go on to commit crimes and escape prosecution.

If the person killed is black, the killer is far more likely to be released. Seventy-three percent of people who killed a black person were released, while 59 percent were released if a white was killed. Cases of justifiable homicide are increasing as defense attorneys progressively use the laws to justify murders as predicted by prosecutors who opposed the introduction of Stand Your Ground laws. Seventy percent of people who invoked "Stand Your Ground" to avoid prosecution were released[32]. In almost one third of cases, the perpetrator initiated the fight, shot an unarmed person or pursued the victim and was still released.

The laws are allowing increasing number of murderers to walk away from charges. Unarmed people have been killed. Some have been killed while lying on the ground, and still others while trying to run away from the gun owner. In one case, a man chased a thief down an alley and killed him with a knife. Increasingly, people's lives are in danger from gun owners who invoke these laws.

Extra-Judicial Murder Incidents

In an incident in 2009 in Fort Myers, Omar Bonilla fired his weapon into the ground and assaulted Demarro Battle. He then went inside and handed his weapon to a friend. Demarro Battle, given the opportunity to retreat, if he were legitimately in fear for his life, instead retrieved a firearm from his vehicle, returned and shot Bonilla three times, including once in the back. He was not charged. In any other country, he could feasibly have been charged with murder, perhaps even premeditated murder, since he had time to plan his actions. The passage of laws like this encourage people to take life instead of using the prudent option, which is to retreat, report the incident to authorities and take the case through the justice system.

The law in Florida often releases men with a history of violence. Maurice Moorer was a man with a history of violence that led to prison sentences over a 2-year period. Yet, he killed his ex-girlfriend's new boyfriend and was released without charge by invoking the Stand Your Ground law [33].

In Milwaukee on May 31st, 2012, Darius Simmons, a 13-year-old boy was shot and killed by his 75-year old neighbor, John Spooner, despite the fact that the boy put up his hands and tried to run away[34]. If the boy had been a few feet closer to the owner's property, or the Stand Your Ground law had been in place in Wisconsin, it is feasible that Spooner would not have been charged with murder. As it is, Spooner was sentenced to life in jail. This begs the question whether the age of a victim plays a part in the right to kill, and whether someone who has plainly given up the fight should still be killed. How this man believed that he was at risk from this young boy is open for debate.

Spooner confronted the boy about stealing shotguns from his home while the teen was retrieving his family's garbage cans from the street. His mother called out to the man to leave the boy alone, but Spooner pulled out a 9mm handgun and shot the child in the chest. Simmons turned and ran and Spooner shot him once more. The boy was reportedly in school at the time the guns were reported stolen. His home was searched and the guns were not found. This child was gunned down for something he did not do.

In one incident, a father was shot in front of his daughter for standing up for children's right to skateboard in a public park. In another, a Florida man chased a thief down an alley and stabbed him to death. In neither incident was the perpetrator charged with a crime.

Impossible Surrender

Even if the victim was retreating, the Stand-Your-Ground law still applies, according to the First Circuit Court of Appeals. In one instance, a man forced his way into a car. Jimmy Hair, a passenger, shot the intruder, Charles E. Harper in the forehead, even as Harper was being dragged away, and no longer presented a threat. The court ruled that Stand Your Ground immunity applies even if the person presenting the threat retreats before the person standing their ground uses their weapon[35].

In another case, two men fell into the water after fighting on a dock. When one of the men, Michael Palmer, climbed out of the water, the other, Timothy McTigue, shot him in the back of the head. He was granted immunity[36]. Palmer was clearly in retreat and unarmed, but a jury found McTigue not guilty.

Carlos Ibanez was acting erratically, doing cartwheels and pounding on doors in an apartment complex. Marcos Antonio Trujillo shot and killed him. Ibanez was not necessarily threatening anyone, but he was killed anyway. His killer was not charged[37].

During a drug deal that turned bad, Anthony Gonzalez was threatened with a gun. Gonzalez chased the man down during a high-speed car chase and killed him. Gonzalez could have retreated but did not; instead he hunted the other man down and killed him. Before Stand Your Ground laws, he would have been charged with murder. As it is, he was only convicted of manslaughter, receiving three years in prison. His lawyer argued that he had a right to be in his car, was licensed to carry a gun and believed his life to be in danger[38].

The victims in these cases have no chance to retreat, to surrender or in any way to mitigate any action they may take. Their lives are forfeit regardless of circumstance. Once embroiled in a given episode, a person has no way to stop being killed. That includes running away, falling on the ground, raising his hands in surrender, calling for help or any indication of his unwillingness to continue. Once in a confrontational situation of any sort, an unarmed person is *de facto* sentenced to death.

Shooting someone in the back, as they are trying to escape has become construed as self-defense. Once someone has raised their hands, fallen to the ground, turned their backs or in any way indicated that they surrender, it can no longer be called self-defense, despite rulings by the courts. In one instance, in a dispute over boating violations, a shooter killed two men. He was released despite having shot the men from over 20 feet away. Neither man touched the shooter at any time. The judge ruled that physical contact was not necessary for the "Stand Your Ground" law to be invoked.

Rules of War

Stand Your Ground laws allow civilians more latitude in the use of force than the U.S. military extends to its soldiers in times of war. VoteVets.org, a veteran's organization, says that these laws are more about the use of force than they are about the right to bear arms. The Rules of Engagement for armed conflict are laid out clearly by the military, and contain a series of clear steps that service members must take in responding to threats. These steps are not laid out for civilians in Stand-Your-Ground states[39].

The steps devised by the military follow a "graduated measure of force".

1. Shouted verbal warning to halt
2. Show your weapon and demonstrate intent to use it
3. Physically restrain, block access, or detain
4. Fire a warning shot if authorized.
5. Shoot to eliminate the threat.

Any service members using undue force after failing to obey these rules are subject to courts martial and charges of manslaughter. The same is clearly not the case within the borders of the United States. Hypothetically, a citizen is safer in Afghanistan than within these borders. If the Trayvon Martin/Zimmerman case had been in Iraq, it is likely that an investigation followed by a charge of manslaughter and compensation for the victims' family would have occurred. In the United States, the killer is immune from prosecution or liability.

In any conflict situation, it is always preferable, and has been the case for centuries that a de-escalation of potential violence is the prudent course of action before someone is killed. Under Stand Your Ground, that standard is overturned. Service members in war cannot hide behind the thought that someone was threatening; they must demonstrate a clear and present danger before using force. Even in the case of a potential threat, steps must be taken to avoid a deadly confrontation. A deadly shooting still requires an investigation. Even the presence of a weapon does not constitute a threat unless there is intent to use that weapon with hostile intent.

Judicial Temerity

Judges must determine cases based on a far lower standard than was previously the case. Judges now determine cases based on the "preponderance of the evidence", rather than on the far stricter, "beyond a reasonable doubt", allowing more defendants to walk free after killing another person.

Leon County Circuit Court Judge Terry P. Lewis wrote,

"Each individual on each side of the exchange of gunfire can claim self-defense. It could conceivably result in all persons who exchanged gunfire on a public street being immune from prosecution."

It now makes prosecuting murder cases almost impossible. The family of a victim receives no justice from the justice system when anyone can claim that they felt a reasonable threat for their lives. It makes a mockery of laws against murder, or aggravated assault.

Additionally, it comes with a cost to the already overburdened court system. An increasing number of cases are being argued using the law, resulting in expensive hearings to decide whether immunity can be applied. William Wiskos applied for immunity after killing his girlfriends' husband. This used a courtroom for an entire day, in addition to the judge, public defender, two prosecutors, clerks and bailiffs and a witness paid $750/hr[40].

Florida: Ignoring the Evidence

A Task Force commissioned by Gov. Rick Scott (R-FL) to study the Stand-Your-Ground law after the Trayvon Martin case ignored several empirical studies that found that these laws lead to a statistically significant increase in justifiable homicides[41]. Other studies have found that these laws impact African Americans to an inordinate degree compared to other population groups. These studies were not incorporated into the panels' final recommendations. The panel determined that people have the right to stand their ground, essentially echoing the words of the statute[42].

Some researchers into the law felt that insufficient data was yet available to make a determination about the law, and legislators used that as evidence to claim that the law is a good law. Rep. Dennis Baxley even claimed that the data supported his contention that the law was not associated with an increase in violent crime[43]. The governors' office says that people have the right to feel safe in Florida and have a fundamental right to stand and defend themselves. Many people are unarmed and do not feel safe because of Stand Your Ground laws. They cannot invoke a fundamental right to stand and defend themselves against gun owners. They now forfeit the right to feel safe from belligerent gun owners.

The researchers' conclusions about the lack of data are correct. Analyses of the data are practically impossible. Prosecutors do not keep records demonstrating how they reached the decision to release suspects, making any research into the laws difficult. There is no trail of how many Stand Your Ground motions have been filed or their outcomes[44]. It is almost impossible to make rational determinations and decisions without adequate data and research into that data.

At least half of the lawmakers on the task force were members of ALEC, the organization that proposed the Stand Your Ground laws to begin with, clearly a blatant conflict of interest. Representative Dennis Baxley was the author of H.B. 249, the statute passed to enact Florida's law. State Senators David Simmons and Gary Siplin were state senators during the unanimous passage of the original bill, while Representative Jason Brodeur was co-sponsor of the bill, and a member of ALEC[45].

Consider the make-up of the committee responsible for choosing the members of the task force. Lt. Gov. Jennifer Carroll, heading the task force was co-sponsor of the house bill and voted in favor in 2005. Selection committee members Senate President Mike Haridopolos and House Speaker Dean Cannon similarly voted in favor of passage. House Speaker Will Weatherford is a member of ALEC. It is unethical to empower a panel to study an issue when the outcome is foreordained by its membership. That is a waste of taxpayer dollars, and makes a mockery of the process. Opponents of the bill were entirely shut out of the selection process, stripping them of the right to free speech and the ability to air their opinions.

There was no formal application process to get onto the committee, and opposition lawmakers were not extended the opportunity to serve. The task force did recommend that some language be clarified to determine what the law means to law enforcement and whether it may encourage vigilantism. It is unlikely that the legislature will act on either of these recommendations.

As someone who does live in Florida, I do not feel safe and secure in Florida, nor do I feel that as an unarmed resident, I have the right to stand my ground against someone that has a gun. It appears that only those that own personal firearms have the right to feel safe and secure. People like me must now live in fear that in any confrontation, I will end up in the morgue. That certainly does nothing to enhance my feeling of safety or security.

The only good thing to come out of the task force is the recommendation that neighborhood watch participants should be limited to observing, not pursuing, confronting or provoking potential suspects. However, the critical injustice at the core of the law has not been addressed at all.

Florida Rep. Alan Williams filed a bill to repeal Florida's law, but it is unlikely to pass the Republicans controlled legislature. Sybrina Fulton, the mother of Trayvon Martin whose unarmed 17-year-old son was killed by George Zimmerman in 2012, joined Williams and state Sen. Dwight Bullard in calling for repeal[46].

Stand Your Ground laws are clearly a legislative and judicial endorsement of modern lynching. It enables people to kill with impunity, secure in the knowledge that they will not have to face a jury or the justice system, or any form of investigation. It creates a new subclass of inferior people, those who do not or are not willing to carry firearms.

The Extra-Judicial Killing of Trayvon Martin

It's 2013 and an American jury just acquitted a man who admitted to stalking and killing an unarmed child. (Richard Dreyfuss)

On the 26th February, 2012, Trayvon Martin, a 17 year old youth was returning to the Sanford townhouse owned by his fathers fiancée with a can of iced tea and packet of Skittles. George Zimmerman, a neighborhood watch volunteer confronted Martin, and after a brief scuffle, gunned him down. Zimmerman was found not guilty in a trial in which he was charged with second-degree murder.

Law enforcement were not charging George Zimmerman with a crime, or even investigating the crime in the immediate aftermath of the incident. They were quite prepared, given their knowledge of the law, to allow Zimmerman to go free without penalty. They claimed that there was no evidence to refute his claim of self-defense. For the same reason, there was equally no evidence to support it. Their inability to investigate the crime, or charge the suspect amounts to gross dereliction of duty to citizens. Taking a life in whatever circumstance is the gravest violation of anyone's civil and human rights; it should be investigated. Over a month after the slaying, Zimmerman still had his gun and his license to carry and use it[1]. Yet, on the 911 recording of the incident, Zimmerman was heard using what sounds like a racial epithet, and saying "he is a black male, something is wrong with him. These a**holes, they always get away."

Zimmerman intentionally followed the victim and confronted him, despite being instructed by a 911 operator to remain in his vehicle. In the confrontation that followed, Zimmerman killed the teenager. No evidence has yet been produced that Trayvon was acting in a suspicious manner, or what constituted this purported suspicious behavior.

Killing the Unarmed

It is clear that Zimmerman chased down an unarmed, black teenager, who was committing no crime and gunned him down. It was Trayvon's right to defend himself against an armed attacker, yet the presence of Zimmerman's firearm assured the revocation of his right. He could credibly have believed his own life to be in danger, and invoked his own right to stand his ground. Since he was unarmed, he could not use that right to his own benefit. His lack of personal protection ultimately led to his death at the hands of a self-professed vigilante.

Zimmerman had no justification for following and accosting the victim, who should have had the right to stand his ground against the perceived threat against him. Trayvon was justified in thinking that his life or body was at risk from Zimmerman. Any rational person will believe that his life is in danger if he is being followed, especially at night in a poorly lit area like the apartment complex in which Martin was killed. Additionally, Martin had every right, under any reasonable law to be where he was and not be accosted by anyone.

Since the teenager was not armed at the time, his only defense against the threat would have been to attack Zimmerman, who had no authority to determine who was permitted to be on the property. Zimmerman took that opportunity to kill the teenager and claim that his own life was in danger. Trayvon Martin is no longer around to dispute the claim, thus his right to stand his ground was infringed. We only have Zimmerman's word that his life was in danger; it is very probable that Trayvon felt that his life was in danger and that he had the right to defend himself against the threat of being gunned down.

Questionable Justification

Zimmerman's life and body was in no danger before he confronted the teenager. He created the incident through his own neuroses and used his paranoia to justify killing Trayvon. As the aggressor, Zimmerman should not have been able to claim self-defense. This only motivates people to use Stand-Your Ground to commit murder and get off without charge. Zimmerman in essence, hunted down the teenager, confronted him over spurious charges that he looked suspicious, and gunned him down, later claiming self-defense, although he did not specifically claim his right under the Stand Your Ground statute.

Consequences of the Verdict

Since Zimmerman managed to beat the charges against him, the probability that people will use deadly force more frequently increases significantly. It will also ensure that defense attorneys use Stand-Your-Ground laws as justification for using lethal force more often. Zimmerman was not charged at first since law enforcement agreed that Zimmerman saw Trayvon as a threat and that this perception was reasonable. Without the benefit of a trial, with all the evidence being presented, law enforcement is unable to determine that the threat was credible. All they had was the word of the assailant as to the sequence of events.

Florida's Reaction to the Martin Case

After the Trayvon Martin case, officials claimed that they would take a close look at the kill-at-will law, but to date, nothing has come to light that indicates they plan to alter the law in any way. The Task Force on Citizens Safety and Protection assembled by

Gov. Rick Scott looking into the killing stated that they ought to "ensure that claims of justifiable homicide are not being granted or denied because of the color of someone's skin"[2]

It has nothing to do with skin color; it has to do with the fact that these laws allow gun owners to kill others with impunity, knowing that they are immune from prosecution, and even from investigation. The task force ought to be looking into whether these laws are violating the rights of victims and of the population in general, particularly that portion of the population that do not carry concealed weapons for protection. Yet, the outcome of the task force investigation was only that the law could stand with a few minor modifications including that the perpetrator not be engaged in any unlawful activity at the time of the incident[3].

Racial Profiling and the Anti-Trayvon Campaign

What is disturbing about the Martin case is the racial bias shown subsequent to the event. Seventy-three percent of African Americans believed that had Trayvon been white, Zimmerman would have been charged[4]. Only 33 percent of whites agreed. Most whites, 52 percent, said that race played no part in the decision. Yet, Zimmerman said plainly on the 911 recording that Trayvon was black, wearing a hoodie and looked suspicious. African Americans justifiably see the killing of the teen as part of the history of injustice leveled at their race, with some comparing it with the killing of Emmett Till, the African American 14-year-old child who was killed in 1955.

In addition to race playing a part in the Trayvon Martin case, perceptions of the youth were also affected by the way he was dressed. Conservative commentator Pat Robertson rebuked the media for portraying Trayvon as a little boy instead of "a fully formed young African American male." According to Robertson, "there's been some crime in this area and the criminals were wearing these hoods so its one of those things."[5] What Trayvon was wearing is ultimately irrelevant, where he was walking is similarly irrelevant. He had every right to be where he was, regardless of what he was wearing, his gender, size, age, color or any other arbitrary attribute. Zimmerman had no knowledge of the young man before the incident, and no right to accost him, regardless of any previous behavior; still less did he have the right to take his life.

Those in positions of privilege, mostly in the white community, can use the laws as a justification for profiling minority groups. Among the white community, many believe that the killing has been politicized and that minorities are clinging to prejudice.

The former general counsel and executive director of the South Carolina Republican Party, Todd Kincannon, tweeted the following[6],

".@DAWNCATHERINE I appreciate you! I agree that Trayvon Martin was a dangerous thug who needed to be put down like a rabid dog".

There is clearly no solid evidence that Trayvon was anything other than a normal young teenager. Yet, a Republican lawmaker demonstrates his racist ideology and prejudice against the victim.

Glenn Beck, the conservative talk show host, claims on his website, The Blaze, that Trayvon might have been an arsonist, a kidnapper, or even a murderer. Beck, noted for his bizarre conspiracy theories has built a significant base within the conservative movement. The editor of the website reported that Martin had been suspended from school, and listed all the reasons he might have been suspended. As it turns out, his suspension was for tardiness[7]. Had he committed any crime listed by Beck, he would likely have been in custody. Even if Trayvon were shown to be any of these things, none should lead to his arbitrary execution. None of this was feasibly known by Zimmerman at the time of the shooting, and thus was irrelevant to the events of that night. Nothing that Trayvon might conceivably have done changes the fact that the teen was killed for no apparent reason. He sounded like a normal, rambunctious teen, and for that he died.

The New York Post produced a headline entitled, "Trayvon Hoodwinked: Tragedy hijacked by race hustlers", specifically naming Al Sharpton and Jesse Jackson as exploiting the incident. They claim that people like Sharpton are inflaming racial passions. The fact is that Zimmerman followed Martin because he was black and looked suspicious. Just as is done all over the country, Martin was being profiled by Zimmerman, and ended up dead as a result.

The Conservative campaign against Trayvon may well have been the deciding factor in the not guilty verdict in the killing. Conservative media launched a media blitz against the teen painting him as a criminal and a drug addict. Without any compelling empirical evidence against the teen, he was just the unfortunate victim of a vigilante act. Painting him in this negative light is the equivalent of blaming a rape victim for causing the rape by wearing a mini skirt or a revealing top. The jury members were feasibly influenced by what they heard and thus violated the sanctity of the jury room.

Reaction from Legislators

State Rep. Dennis Baxley, who sponsored the Florida law together with State Senator Durell Peadon, both members of ALEC, worked closely with NRA lobbyist Marion Hammer, says[8]

"A lot of the data shows that it has been very effective in protecting people from harm and acts of violence".

Plainly, that cannot be said of Trayvon Martin, who was guilty of no crime other than trying to protect himself from harm, especially when attacked by someone far heavier, far stronger, and armed. These laws do not protect people from violence if any altercation can be used as an excuse to exploit the provisions of the acts. It places far more people in harms way, and legitimizes homicide.

Baxley also said, "It's a clear position that we will stand with victims of violent attacks when the law is in their favor," He continued, "People want to know we stand on the side of victims of crime instead of the side of criminals." In the case of Stand Your Ground, the victims, those that are killed by gun owners, are most often not criminals involved in criminal activities. Trayvon Martin was not a criminal, just an innocent teen. The law protects gun owners, not their victims. Conservatives are redefining what constitutes a violent attack, in which even the perception of violence is punished by death.

Profiting from Tragedy

What makes the incident even more distressing is the reaction of some in the gun industry. An online gun retailer, the Hiller Armament Company of Virginia, promoted an advertisement for range targets that resemble the 17-year old youth[9]. The target shows a hooded figure holding skittles and iced tea with the cross hairs of a target on his chest[10]. The seller reportedly wanted to make money off the controversy and sold his entire stock in two days. The lack of empathy and hate mongering shown towards the memory and the family of a victim of what amounted to a heinous crime and a travesty of justice are of great concern. The sellers claim, "They support Zimmerman and believe he is innocent and that he shot a thug."[11]

The gun lobby claims that they are responsible, yet statements and actions like this cannot be portrayed as responsible. It makes a mockery of this young man's death. When innocent black youths, returning from the store are thought of as thugs, without any compelling empirical evidence, it is reasonable to assume racist intent. This is commercial exploitation of a horrific event, in which a young man who had done no wrong was gunned down in his own apartment complex.

Homicide Without Trial

It is a travesty of justice that Zimmerman was released without charge on the night he killed Trayvon. Without the demand by Martins family and by social media for justice, the case would not have gone to court. As it is, it took months for the police to finally charge Zimmerman with Second Degree Murder. Evidence that should have been collected on the night in question was lost due to the shoddy dereliction of duty displayed by local law enforcement.

At the very least a criminal trial should have been the outcome from the start. Zimmerman took this human life without compunction or apparent remorse. In addition, the family ought to have had the right to redress of grievances in the civil court system. Taking that right away by statute should be seen as a grave violation of the families First Amendment right to free speech.

What is even more disturbing is the number of people who donated to Zimmerman's defense fund. They were supporting this man, without any compelling evidence, other than his word, and defending an unjust and ill-conceived law.

Absence of Evidence or Testimony

What is of equal concern in the Trayvon case is that Zimmerman did not testify in his own defense. A jury cannot determine whether he acted in self-defense or not without his testimony. No one else was there. Anything anyone else said was hearsay or circumstantial evidence. Zimmerman claimed self-defense, but did not show or demonstrate self-defense by not testifying. If he was attacked as he claims, he should not have been reluctant to testify. The fact that the jury claimed that Trayvon was the aggressor, in the complete absence of any compelling empirical evidence, appears to show jury bias.

There was no way to prove that Trayvon was the aggressor, and by finding for Zimmerman, this is what they claimed. The jury took the position that Trayvon attacked Zimmerman and Zimmerman was entitled to defend himself. However, there was no way for them to know this, unless Zimmerman testified in his own defense. This is where Stand Your Ground laws fail the taste test. The law is taking the word of someone who has perpetrated a criminal act over the non-existent word of a dead victim. The justice system clearly failed Trayvon Martin, his family, non-gun owners, and the African American community.

Trayvon had every right to be in that apartment complex, and Zimmerman did not have the right to challenge that right, or to take away Martins right to be there or expropriate his right to life. By confronting him, he was *ipso facto* removing Martin's right to be there unhindered or harassed by an armed vigilante.

Despite the Trayvon Martin killing, Marion Hammer still insists that

> "Officials should not be stampeded by emotionalism...This law is not about one incident. There is absolutely nothing wrong with the law."

It is always about one case, one case at a time, for if law perpetuates injustice, it is a bad law for the individual or for the group. Perhaps Hammer should ask Trayvon if he believes that people should be forbidden from expressing emotion, or outrage at the outcome. The law does nothing useful; but it does legitimize murder or extra judicial killing and by that token is an abuse of legislative power. It is also a crime against humanity, and should be punished as such.

Schools, Children and Gun Massacres

Whenever there is news of a terrible shooting, I wonder why America has so miserably failed to enact even common-sense gun regulation (Jon Meacham)

The Schools Are to Blame

A favorite tactic of gun proponents is to blame the school curriculum for school massacres or general gun violence. Variously blaming evolution, teachers unions, or the absence of God in classrooms is another attempt to mislead or change the subject from guns to anything else.

Violence and bullying can happen in schools and children can become resentful and sometimes commit violent acts. What is more to blame than the curriculum is the reluctance of parents and school administrators to approach bullying and violence and find ways to prevent them before they become a problem. Guns are a problem in certain schools, especially in areas with high rates of poverty. Many children who have been threatened with a firearm, or have seen someone injured or killed by children armed with guns may feel compelled to defend themselves, and find a way to bring firearms into schools.

Some parents may see the solution to school violence as home schooling, but this may paradoxically make the problem worse. Children learn social skills in a school environment, and learn to deal with hostility and confrontation, something that they cannot do in the home. Schools also enable children to mix with people from different social strata, something that is unlikely to happen in the closed environment of the home school. Chance meetings of public school students outside the home can lead to confrontation if the home schooled student is not seen as a member of the community, especially in areas with high levels of poverty.

Seeing a need to home school children because of school violence is a reflection of the culture of fear and paranoia carefully nurtured by the gun industry. A society with fewer firearms would not have children taking firearms to school for self-defense through fear, or to harm their classmates. This problem is just not a feature of schools in other developed nations, and it does not have to be one here. A society living in fear of itself is not a society that can grow and prosper successfully; it needs to address intractable problems.

Schools are among the safest places in the nation. Far less violence happens in schools than happens in other public spaces. Homes can be violent places for far too many children, and when a child is home schooled in a violent home, the abuse may never be noticed. If that same child attended a public school it is far more likely that domestic abuse could be brought to the attention of authorities. Students who are home schooled are more likely to be in a home with firearms, and thus far more likely to be harmed by those firearms than they are in a school shooting. Home-schooled children may also find themselves in a far more controlling and authoritarian environment than they might find in a school. Home schooling can easily become a tightly controlled social setting from which it is difficult to escape.

What is absurd is that schools are now spending funds that would be better spent on instruction and teachers on providing bulletproof whiteboards for classroom use. The University of Maryland Eastern shore is spending $60,000 on high tech tablets that professors can use to protect themselves. Some manufacturers are promoting bulletproof inserts for children's backpacks[1]. The gun culture is producing paranoia in otherwise sensible people, and quite possibly the onset of PTSD or similar maladies in children. This is all to support an extremist pro gun lobby.

The Lack of God in Schools

For the most part, European nations keep religion out of the public sphere, and yet they have few deaths by gun. In comparison, the United States is far more religious, and has a far higher rate of gun death. Any rational person must conclude that the presence of God or religious belief is more likely to lead to gun deaths than secular belief. Perhaps we should reduce religious influences in order to reduce gun deaths.

Rep Louie Gohmert (R-TX) claimed,

> "The shootings could have been avoided if the country placed a higher value on God."

Mike Huckabee, Baptist minister and Fox News commentator, hours after the Newtown shootings said this,

> "We ask why there is violence in our schools, but we have systematically removed God from our schools. Should we be so surprised that schools would become a place of carnage? Maybe we ought to let God in on the front end and we wouldn't have to call him to show up when its all said and done on the back end."

Huckabee needs to explain a number of church shootings. In a building specifically built to worship God, by his logic, there should be no shootings at all. Consider for instance the mass shootings in a Sikh temple in Oak Creek, Wisconsin. The six people killed and the four wounded were worshipping in their own way. The Daingerfield Church shooting in Texas cost the lives of five people and wounded ten others[2]. Perhaps they were not praying enough. At the Knoxville Unitarian Universalist Church, motivated by a desire to kill liberals and Democrats, a man killed two and injured seven others[3]. None of these incidents was caused by a lack of God in churches.

Huckabee had similar words after the Aurora tragedy,

> "We don't have a crime problem, a gun problem or a violence problem. What we have is a sin problem. And since we have ordered God out of our schools, and communities, the military and public conversations, you know we really shouldn't act surprised...when all hell breaks loose."

Again, Huckabee attempts to justify massacres with an appeal to a nebulous and ill-defined sin, instead of being courageous enough to tackle firearm possession. Attempts like these intend to mislead or misdirect attention away from the proximate cause of gun violence and place the blame on the indistinct concept of sin and evil. By that measure, any problem in society might be ascribed to sin and evil rather than to people's policies.

If we as a society limited access to extreme weapons, it would be a lot more difficult for the sinful to commit their atrocities. This society clearly has a gun problem that exacerbates violence and crime, and conservative commentators are unwilling to tackle that problem. Blaming sin just ignores the problem and ascribes it so something other than its true cause.

Huckabee shares his sentiments with that icon of Muslim tolerance, Iran's Supreme Leader, Ali Khamenei, who similarly announced, *"a lack of religion in the United States is the main reason for the school shooting[4]."*

Brian Fisher of the American Family Association on prayer in public schools,

> "God is not going to go where he is not wanted. Now we have spent 50 years telling God to get lost. Telling God, we do not want you in our schools, we don't want to pray to you in our schools, we don't want to pray to you before football games, we don't want to pray to you at graduation, we don't want anyone talking to you in a graduation speech. We have kicked God out of our public school system. And I think God would say to us, 'Hey, I'll be glad to protect our children but you've gotta invite me back into your world first. I'm not gonna go where I'm not wanted. I'm a gentleman."

Fisher clearly makes a mockery of the God he professes to worship. No one ever claimed that God was not wanted in schools, just that there is a time and a place for worship, and no one has the right to impose that time and place on others, especially in a place dedicated to education. I highly doubt that a Creator who managed to create a Universe is likely to care whether He is allowed on school property. For anyone to claim that twenty children and six adults were slaughtered on school property because God was sulking about not being allowed on that property, or to punish the children, is offensive.

People like Huckabee should stop putting words into God's mouth, or claiming to speak for God, just to justify the possession of extreme weapons. To suggest that God abandoned these children because they could not worship is equally without empathy, shows an indifference to their suffering, and portrays God as vindictive, petty and unmerciful. No God worthy of worship would sacrifice twenty children and six adults on the Second Amendment altar, or because of secularism, abortion or lack of prayer in society. Only one conjured by the inhumanity of an ideology that promotes the possession of extreme weaponry and the callous indifference to the deaths of children.

James Dobson of the organization "Focus on the Family,

"Because we have turned out back on Scripture and on God Almighty, I think he has allowed judgment to fall upon us. I think that's what's going on."

Again, there is little empathy emanating from Dobson, who appears to justify the slaughter in Newtown with an appeal to God's judgment. Perhaps he would be better served in the service of Kali or some equally unpleasant supernatural force. The slaughter in Newtown was a time to mourn for the children, and circumscribe firearms, not advance an unpleasant and intolerant religious agenda.

The lack of compassion continued unabated, with WND, a conservative news site proclaiming that America should *"expect more Sandy Hooks, not fewer, because of America's secularism and restriction on guns"*. Co-opting God to support the Second Amendment, when a great number of religious organizations support stricter gun regulation and a concentration on reducing gun violence is similarly unwarranted and mixes an earthly possession with spiritual beliefs. WND sounds as though it relishes the idea that God would punish society by permitting the slaughter of twenty children and their teachers.

The Westboro Baptist Church announced plans to picket the funerals of the children killed in Sandy Hook to sing praise to God for the glory of his work in executing his judgment. The group targeted Connecticut's gay marriage legislation as the cause of the Newtown massacre. The group clearly blames God for executing twenty children and their teachers because the Creator of the Universe was unable to find another way to show His displeasure. How small and petty they must believe their God to be, that He would punish those who had nothing to do with gay marriage legislation. It is more likely that they are promoting their own intolerant politico-religious agenda.

The fact is that the obsession with owning extreme weapons and the total refusal to countenance even the most mild of gun regulation is what caused the massacre in Newtown, and it is that obsession, not God, that is to blame.

Armed Guards at Schools

The NRA ran an ad after the Sandy Hook shooting complaining that even though President Obama's children have armed guards at their school, Democrats oppose similar measures at schools countrywide. They clearly do not understand the idea that the

President, regardless of who he might be, is always under threat from radicals that wish to do harm to he and his family. The security officers for the Presidents children tend to be armed with personal side arms, which would be quite ineffective against a concerted attack from people armed with assault weapons. Children in general do not have the problem that people are intent on killing them for political gain, whereas the President's children do.

In a spate of political absurdity, Vice President Joe Biden actually agreed that funds should be set aside to provide schools with security. The crime bill he penned in 1994 included a provision for placing police officers in schools. Rep. Mark Meadows (R-NC) introduced legislation to restore funding for the Cops in Schools program allowing local law enforcement to hire officers for school duty.

The very idea of armed guards at schools is unworkable. Consider that there were 98,817 public schools in the United States in the 2010-2011 school year[5]. This includes charter, regular, special needs, vocational and magnet schools. If we were to place a single armed guard in every school, at a median salary of $55,010 per annum[6] excluding perquisites, this would amount to some $5.4Bn per year. The NRA has called for "*sworn law enforcement personnel*", rather than security guards, which accounts for the cost[7]. This does not include the costs of equipping and arming these officers. Additionally, these guards need to take breaks to eat or drink, or deal with altercations on the grounds, at which time they would be away from their posts. They also need to take vacations, or they may fall ill, which means finding and funding replacements.

There were also 33,366 private schools in the same school year, which would increase the required expenditure by $1.8Bn to $7.2Bn each year, to prevent 23 school homicides each year. If we were to require at least two officers per school for the abovementioned reasons, costs double to \$14.5Bn. Most campuses are open between 7 a.m. and 9 p.m., requiring at least two shifts of at least two officers each[8]. That would effectively double the cost again to \$29Bn. That amounts to more than \$1Bn per homicide.

The cost of surveillance equipment, transportation around larger campuses and uniforms also needs to be considered. The cost of perquisites, vacations, payroll taxes, offices and computers must be included. In addition to that, costs for training SRO's to deal with children, and constitutional protections for children must be included. This says nothing about the support staff required, supervisors, and background checks for new hires. If private firms provide security services, those firms require fees in addition to the officers that they provide, again increasing costs.

Each of the more than 200,000 officers hired for schools would need to be armed and equipped with the accoutrements of security including ammunition, firearms training, bullet proof vests, uniforms and surveillance equipment, all of which is wonderful for the security industry and does nothing to improve the security of school children.

A Guard in Every Classroom

The NRA has even suggested putting armed guards in every classroom. One wonders whether they have thought through the massive cost burden placed on the budget at a time when conservatives want to slice the national debt. They are firing teachers, and closing schools, but they want to waste more funding on security guards in every classroom. This would effectively double employment costs while education budgets are being slashed, and do nothing either to change the security situation in schools or to improve the quality of education.

The cost of uniforms, firearms, extra seating in each classroom, and training would destroy the education budget. This would probably suit conservatives, since their strategy is ultimately to destroy public education, and at the same time, they could provide a massive inflow of cash to the arms industry. None of which would solve the problem of gun violence, not just in schools, but also around the country.

Ironically, the task force commissioned by the NRA to develop the school shield program was headed by Asa Hutchinson, who conveniently sits on the board of Pinkerton Government Services, subsidiary of one of the nations largest private security contractors, Securitas[9]. Were government mandated SRO's introduced in schools, Securitas would benefit to the tune of hundreds of millions of dollars.

Actions of Killers at Schools

Since an armed guard cannot be in all places at once, and schools cover a large area of land, with many events or classes at any given time, a single guard is insufficient to cover the entire school. That would entail having multiple guards, at least one at each entrance and exit, growing costs incrementally.

An attacker, knowing that there is at least one armed guard at a school will take one of several courses of action. First, he may attempt to neutralize the guard, causing another casualty. He might wait until the guard is elsewhere on the property to gain entrance. He could find an alternative entrance to the one at which the guard is posted. He could conceal his weapons on his person and enter the facility, or hide the weapons before or after classes when there is no armed guard.

There were armed guards at two of the schools at which there were massacres, Virginia Tech and Columbine in Colorado. At neither school was the armed guard able to prevent the massacres. In the Fort Hood, Texas shooting at an army base, despite the enormous number of armed and trained personnel, the shooter was able to kill with impunity. In the Columbine School shooting, arriving police did not stop the shooters, rather they secured the perimeter, while the two perpetrators killed themselves[10]. Virginia Tech has an entire police department to deal with the 30,000 students at the campus. They did nothing to prevent or hinder the killer. In Columbine, the uniformed community resource officer was having lunch with the schools unarmed security officer when the shooting happened[11].

In a shootout between security guards and killers, there will doubtless be collateral damage to students caught in the crossfire. There is no guarantee that security guards would be able to apprehend or prevent shootings, and may cause more death and injury attempting to stop the killers. Shooters, even skilled police officers caught in live-fire situations often fire wildly and excessively, creating hazards to bystanders and innocent civilians.

Cutting School Budgets and Arming Teachers

Wayne LaPierre, NRA chief had this to say,

"With all the foreign aid that the United States does [sic] with all the money in the federal budget, can't we afford to put a police officer in every single school?"

Conservatives have been cutting back on funds for schools and for teachers, who are essential to the smooth running of the schools. Now, instead of funding for education, which is the object of the exercise, society will expend those funds on armed guards. This also creates an unpleasant learning environment for children who see themselves as being under siege by roving gunmen. It would be far better for their development if they could grow up in a safe environment unconcerned about violent gun owners.

The alternative proposal is to have teachers arm themselves on school property. There are many reasons that this is unworkable and unreasonable. Firstly, teachers are in the business of educating their children, not tackling violent gun owners intent on massacring children. Most teachers are women, often smaller women who did not get into the business of educating children to act as law enforcement officers.

Many teachers are afraid of firearms, do not have the training to handle firearms, especially around children, and are not willing to carry firearms. Additionally, it sends a poor message to children to have a teacher armed in the classroom. It creates a siege mentality that is not conducive to learning. A teacher has to move around a classroom, which means carrying the weapon with them at all times. Leaving the weapon lying around is an accident waiting to happen, especially with curious children.

Assault Weapons for Teachers

Some in the pro-gun lobby want teachers to have assault weapons, which is an even greater logistical nightmare for the teachers. The weapon would have to be secured at all times from children; they could not be carried around in classrooms. Children would live in an artificially induced atmosphere of fear and paranoia. Accidents are almost inevitable in this environment, causing even more deaths.

These weapons would probably be kept in classrooms, which makes them a wonderful source of guns for potential criminals, or mischievous or aggressive children. Young males especially in upper classes could easily overpower a teacher and take these weapons for use on their own classmates. Significant amounts of money would need to be spent on secure facilities for these armaments, reducing the amounts spent on actually educating children. What this country does not need is a militaristic society in which everything from school onwards revolves around fear and guns.

The very presence of guns in classrooms may increase the level of aggression or defiance towards authority, as has been found in other studies on the effects of firearm presence on attitude. These guns could encourage children to test the resolve of teachers, and could lead to violent confrontations.

There is also nothing to suggest that teachers themselves could not be the source of the gun violence. Teachers, like everyone else in society are prone to jealousy, resentments or anger, which may manifest at any time. It would be far too easy for teachers to use those weapons against their own pupils, or other teachers.

Militarized Schools and the School-Prison Pipeline

There is also the perception that schools are being militarized, especially in poorer districts populated mostly by people of color. There are fears that this will drive the school-to-prison pipeline, leading youths to unnecessarily end up embroiled in the justice system. There is already a tendency to overuse police officers in schools, arresting children as young as five for meaningless "crimes" such as kissing another student or brandishing a toy gun. In Mississippi, children have been arrested for showing up to school late or wearing the wrong color socks[12].

African-Americans are far more likely to be suspended for behaviors such as "defiance" or "disorderly conduct" than white children who tend to be suspended for cutting classes or graffiti. Black boys are three times more likely to be suspended than whites and black girls four times more likely to be suspended than white girls. Armed guards in schools are far more likely to be used as implicit threats against minority populations than for preventing gun violence.

Schools are becoming a gateway used to shepherd vulnerable populations, invariably African American and Latino, into the prison system. Installing officers in schools will undoubtedly lead to the imposition of police-state tactics on vulnerable children and teens. Installing guards at schools will only exacerbate the zero-tolerance policies used in schools due to the war on drugs and socially conservative policies.

Criminalizing School Populations

Students in schools with School Resource Officers were 2.9 times more likely to be arrested and 4.7 times more likely to be charged with disorderly conduct[13] than schools without. This criminalizes the student body and increases the probability of students dropping out of school. Far from preventing school violence, it is more likely that such policies increase resentment towards authority in general and the school system in particular, creating a greater criminal and gun problem, and a societal problem[14].

Rather than assisting students or improving behavior, these demonstrably failed policies have devastating consequences for students[15]. Children who should end up in the principals' office now end up at the local precinct being charged with crimes. The presence of SRO's is likely to lead school administration to resort to excessive punishments for students instead of relying on reasonable remedies for misdemeanors. SRO's, who are often drawn from the ranks of law enforcement, are more likely to treat infractions as criminal actions. Schools ought to be sanctuaries in which children learn about their society, how to act in society and to prepare them for full entry into that society, not as a holding pen for future criminals[16].

Surveillance of Students

There is also the danger that children perceived as being a problem or a threat will be monitored by threat assessment teams set up in each school, which not only violates liberties, but also creates a sense of paranoia in both teachers and students. Schools become little more than authoritarian mini-states or penal colonies having more in common with George Orwell's '1984' than institutes of learning. The NRA wants to create security zones throughout schools consisting of physical security barriers and surveillance systems, dramatically raising the cost of running schools, with very little benefit for the community.

The 'Zero Tolerance' policies introduced during the drug war turned schools into battlegrounds for policies that treat underage students as fodder for the juvenile justice system. The idea that we categorize people as children for good reason, namely that they are insufficiently mature to fully understand the ramifications of their actions was lost in the fog of overzealous intolerance towards any and all regulatory infractions, including disorderly conduct[17].

In Jefferson County, Alabama, 96% of students referred to juvenile courts were referred for misdemeanor offenses or violations[18]. Of misdemeanor referrals, 29% were for disorderly conduct. The introduction of SRO's in all schools would likely lead to the same intolerance and the ideological creation of schools as armed encampments. Targeting and charging students for disruptive rather than criminal behavior is not conducive to a safe school environment.

The NRA even suggests monitoring schoolwork for violent fantasies that may signal impending violent acts. The very tenets of free speech, for which institutes of learning are supposed to be havens, are undermined by such actions. Additionally, teachers are not qualified to determine whether schoolwork reveals violent intentions. The NRA goes further than this and insists on monitoring social media sites for threats. While the NRA rails against tyrannical government and governmental intrusion on their rights, they are quite prepared to impose those same restrictions and intrusions on school children using extremely low probability events as justification.

Institutes of Learning or Paranoia

The paranoia created by the gun lobby's insistence on firearms everywhere in society is not conducive to a healthy learning environment in schools. The gun lobby created the gun problem and now needs to turn to dramatic remedies like creating fortified schools to resolve the situation. Instead of getting rid of the firearms, they want to create a militarized state and a society saturated with armed men. All this does is to create a neurotic, nervous community in which firearms are used to solve problems, and does nothing to foster an open and free society.

Instead of using schools as scaled down imitations of concentration camps, we should be using more funds to actually educate children. Firearms should be kept as far away from schools as humanly possible by increasing the cordon of the gun free zone to include homes and businesses that surround schools. The idea of militarizing schools to prevent the 20 homicides in schools each year amounts to yet another unnecessary conservative-gun-industry inspired boondoggle on the same order as the infamous southern border fence and its associated army of border guards.

Even if schools were militarized to this extent, killers would just find extra-mural activities to target, including football, basketball or baseball games, in which large numbers of students are gathered conveniently in the same place. The carnage would be even worse than it would be within the school buildings.

Gun-Free Zones

Wayne LaPierre blamed gun free zones for the killing in Sandy Hook,

> "Politicians pass laws for gun-free zones, they issue press releases bragging about them ... in so doing they tell every insane killer in America that schools are the safest place to inflict maximum mayhem with minimum risk."

The gun lobby blamed gun free school zones for the Newtown killings, and yet gun free zones in schools have been spectacularly successful in preventing gun crimes. Schools are among the safest places for children to be anywhere in the nation. Gun violence and homicide is lower in schools than any other public place. Children feel safer in schools than anywhere else, and yet the gun lobby wants to convert schools into prisons with armed guards.

School violence has declined dramatically over the last two decades[19]. Between 1995 and 2005, there were 255 homicides of youths aged 5 to 18 in schools, or 23 per year, compared with the more than 10,000 homicides each year across the country[20]. In 2009, there were 17 homicides in schools nationwide[21]. School homicides represent about 0.2% of total homicides. Violence in school is given far wider media coverage than violence in other locales, giving parents the impression that there is more violence than there actually is.

The chance of violent death among juveniles is about 40 times as great outside school as it is in school[22]. The school homicide rate is around one per million, far lower than the overall homicide rate. During the 2009/2010 school year, the odds of the homicide of a child at a school or school related event was one in 2.5 million, as compared to the odds of being killed in a motor vehicle accident, which was one in 16,000[23].

Judging by the low number of school homicides, which amount to some 297 since 1980[24], gun-free zones have made schools far safer than anywhere else in the nation. If these zones were extended to the entire country, gun homicides would feasibly plummet, gun injuries would follow and the associated costs would decline dramatically.

Despite the evidence, Steve Stockman, (R-TX) wants to repeal the federal law prohibiting firearms in school zones. The consequence of his demands is a likely increase in the number of firearm deaths in and around schools[25]. Stockman is working with Gun Owners of America to introduce this legislation, completely disregarding the fact that school homicide is almost non-existent.

There is scant evidence to suggest that killers in mass shootings choose their targets purely because they are gun-free zones. There is evidence to suggest that the targets are chosen because of resentment or a grievance towards some attribute of the target. Workplace shootings inevitably happen because of a firing, downsizing, or other resentment towards employers or colleagues. Such things as bullying, isolation or alienation from peers or school authorities are likely triggers for school place shootings. The white supremacist that targeted the Sikh temple was driven by racism, or religious intolerance not the fact that it was a gun free zone. What makes these killings easier is the gathering together of large numbers of people in one place, not gun free zones.

Since most mass shooters kill themselves soon after committing their acts, they are certainly not looking for a gun free zone. Their intent is murder-suicide; it does not particularly matter to them whether guns are present or not. If gun free zones were more attractive invitations to mass killers, there would almost certainly be far more homicides than the average 9 school homicides per year since 1980. In one study, only 12 of the nation's 62 mass shootings occurred in schools, 20 in workplaces and the rest in shopping malls, restaurants, religious and government buildings[26].

Education Instead of Gun Regulation

Gun groups make the claim that educating people about firearms would suffice to prevent gun crimes. Programs like the Eddie Eagle Gun Safe program, taught by the NRA, are used as programs to entice people to buy and use firearms, not prevent them from using firearms.

The premise of the NRA program is that children should stop, don't touch, leave the area, and tell an adult if they encounter a firearm. What the program misses is that children are not automatons or programmable robots; they are young people with active, inquisitive minds. The first thing that most children will do when faced with a firearm, regardless of what they have been told, is to handle the firearm to determine whether what they have been told is valid. It is also highly likely that the first thing they will do is turn the firearm around and stare down its barrel, a guarantee of almost certain death.

The NRA program glamorizes firearms, making them forbidden fruit, something that only adults are allowed to use. Nothing could be more enticing to a child than to find a firearm when an adult is not around. It is better to ensure that children have no access to firearms by keeping them out of homes with children. Keeping firearms openly in a home with children ought to be seen as a form of child abuse and punished as such. The chances of a child being killed in a home with a firearm are vastly greatly than in homes without firearms.

A program designed to inform children of the extreme dangers of firearms, the lives lost to gun violence and the people injured beyond repair by firearms would be far more useful than the glamorized image of firearms produced by NRA programs. Informing children about the dangers of using firearms to resolve conflict, instead using anger management and conflict resolution, would be far more useful. The NRA programs are used to encourage children to become involved in the gun community rather than keep them away from firearms. It is used as a platform to promote and advertise gun usage and the gun community, rather than impress upon children the dangers inherent in firearms and their ownership.

Education is not going to help the battered wife whose husband is about to kill her with a firearm, or the victim of a drive by shooting, or the kid who takes a gun to school because he is afraid of bullies or gang members. The gun lobby claims that education will stop gun violence, without a clear understanding of the underlying dynamic of gun violence and what causes it. A gun owner in a blind rage is unlikely to consult a manual telling him to calm down. Education programs that glamorize gun ownership are ultimately harmful to the children they are supposed to help.

While conservatives and their pro-gun allies are pushing for gun education programs in schools, they are busy cutting funding for essential education programs like music, art appreciation, and gym class, all of which are far more likely to improve a child's life than are firearms. There are many subjects that we could teach children to improve the planet, rather than handing them the instrument of violence and destruction. The way to improve a child's chances of success in life is to extend to them the education that will prepare them to earn a reasonable living. That will not be accomplished with a firearm.

It is ironic that the gun lobby wants gun education, and yet they refuse to allow the CDC to study the reasons behind gun violence and the ways in which that violence can be mitigated. The gun lobby claims to want to know what happened and why, and yet prevent government agencies from studying the problem of gun violence.

Blaming Parents for Gun Violence

Mitt Romney, presumptive presidential candidate, blamed single parents for gun violence, since he believed that children should grow up in two parent homes, while Rick Santorum said that single mothers were "breeding more criminals"[27]. One editorial that I read suggested that massacres happen because killers think it is acceptable behavior. The writer suggests that killers do not respect life in their "quest for dominance". The writer believed that respect has to "be taught at home...a child learns how to respect other people by watching their parents"[28].

This is typical of the vague and inconsequential non-solution that has driven the gun industry for decades. We could use the same argument about other social depravities, including spouse or child abuse, rape, or other forms of violence. We need solid solutions to gun violence, and it is up to society to find these solutions, not solely up to parents to reprimand their children. This is an individualistic solution to a complex problem producing nothing more than more gun violence.

An NBC poll finds that most people blame parents for gun violence rather than free access to guns[29]. It is highly unbelievable that American parents are less responsible, or worse, than parents in other countries are. This fosters the belief that society should trust that parents are going to do the right thing rather than the society attempting to solve problems. We are putting the lives of vulnerable children in the hands of people who may or may not be responsible and handing them the means to do potential harm to their children.

Violent Video Games

Conservatives favor bans on virtual guns in video games and the reduction of violence in those games. These weapons are virtual, the fighters and their opponents are virtual. This is fake gun violence and has no bearing on reality. Even children understand the difference between movies, video games, and real life firearms, which do actual harm.

Wayne LaPierre, in his first appearance in public after the Newtown shootings, chose to place the blame for the massacre on the makers of violent video games.

> "There exists in this country a callous, corrupt and corrupting shadow industry that sells, and sows, violence against its own people through vicious, violent video games with names like Bulletstorm, Grand Theft Auto, Mortal Kombat and Splatterhouse."

The NRA has produced a video game called *"NRA Gun Club"*, which has an E-rating for children older than 10. It involves shooting at a number of different items, including watermelons, bottles and clay pigeons using a variety of brand name firearms. This video as produced by the same company, Crave Entertainment, which produced a game called *"Trigger Man"*, involving a mob hit man[30].

LaPierre did not explain why Japan has no gun massacres. Japan as a nation spends more on video games ($44 per capita in the U.S., versus $55 in Japan) than the United States. Japan's gun death rate is so low it is hardly worth mentioning in comparison to that in the United States. The rate of gun ownership per 100 people is 0.6 in Japan as against 88 in the U.S. Japan is also one of the safest, most peaceful nations on Earth, despite their love of violent video games. The reason for the higher death rate in the U.S. is patently obvious.

All around the world, people play the same, violent video games, yet the gun death rate is low in Europe, the Far East, Australia, and Canada. Clearly, violent video games did not cause Adam Lanza, the Connecticut shooter, to become a mass killer. All the nations or geographical areas mentioned have few or no massacres. All of them have stringent gun regulations. The United States has a great number of massacres and large numbers of guns. The conclusions are inescapable.

Violence in the developed world has been dropping for more than a decade, a decade during which video games made their debut and became a social phenomenon. Using the NRA argument it could be claimed that playing violent video games actually prevents violence in society. Violence has not increased during that time, and murder rates are declining.

The U.S. Supreme Court ruled that the effects of violent video games on children are "both small and indistinguishable from effects produced by other media." In their ruling in *Brown v. Entertainment Merchants Association*, the Court dismissed the charge that video games influences actual violence in society. The Court also addressed hypocrisy in the California legislature, which wanted restrictions on video games while still allowing violent movies.

There is some evidence to suggest that violent video games are linked to aggressive behavior, for instance by fostering the belief that the use of aggression to resolve conflict is more effective than other methods, and that the world is a frightening place[31]. We need to know what effect the use of real ammunition and firearms on a shooting range has on gun owners. It is feasible that shooting ranges encourage violent and aggressive behavior, or desensitizes gun owners to violence, which suggests that we ought to ban shooting ranges.

Gun Lobby's Hypocrisy on Violent Video Games

It seems a little hypocritical of the gun lobby to criticize the video game industry. It is infinitely better for children to sit in front of a TV screen killing fake opponents than to be out on a shooting range or killing animals in the wild. The lives children take playing video games are virtual ones, rather than the very real lives taken while hunting. Indeed, when a gun owner takes his weapons to a firing range, he is often shooting at depictions of humans, albeit in silhouette, with live ammunition, not with virtual lasers or firearms. These targets often show prejudicial and racist depictions of criminal elements, which serve to intensify societal divisions.

The violence sold and sown by the gun industry is far more real and infinitely more devastating to the lives of the tens of thousands killed and injured each year than the productions of the video game industry. The corruption produced by gun industry financed political campaigns is also far more egregious than the small amounts supplied by the video game industry. The lives lost to gun violence around the world is infinitely greater than those lost to violence aggravated by video games or movies.

Children at greatest risk for psychological trauma are those who experience gun violence first hand, or see the results in their neighborhoods or schools. Video games may play some part in social attitudes among youth, but experiencing real violence has a far greater impact. The video games available to children have become more graphic and more violent over the last two decades, and yet youth violence is declining[32].

Violent Media as a Predictor of Violent Crime

One study found that exposure to violent games was not predictive of violent crime. Rather, predictive traits were family violence exposure, gender and innate aggression[33]. Exposure to violent movies or video games may be an aggravating factor, along with other factors, but not predictive or indicative of violence on its own. While playing violent video games appears to increase aggressive thoughts, one study suggests that there is little evidence to suggest that this results in either short or long-term changes in violent behavior[34]. It appears more likely that genetic or nurtured predisposition leads to aggressive childhood temperament and aggressive adult personality. Aggressive personalities are more likely to resort to aggression during times of stress.

There is also the open question, as with violent movies, whether certain personality types are drawn to violent video games. The violent actions that they display or in which they participate may relate more to their personality types than the entertainment medium they choose, but it is their innate predisposition for violence that is to blame, rather than the medium itself. In the absence of that medium, they might feasibly have chosen some other form of violence. The interaction between an already aggressive personality and violent video games may be predictive of violent crime[35]. The suggestion of the study is that aggressive or violent personalities actively seek out examples of violence, or show a preference for violent entertainment.

There is also the fact that, given the ubiquitous nature of video games, any particular massacre or incidence of gun violence may include regular video game players as perpetrators. That does not indicate that the video games influenced the incidence of violence in any way, any more than the consumption of Cheerios in the morning is predictive of violence. There may be some long-term effects of violent entertainment, which along with other aggravating factors may influence violent acts. Hypothetically, individuals may become desensitized to violence, develop a lack of empathy, and more easily plan or perpetrate violent acts.

Society should question whether violent video games, movies and extreme weapons should be kept away from people with inherent violent or aggressive personalities. It may well be that, as with violent entertainment, people with a predisposition to violence are drawn to extreme weapons, and that society should not trust those who pursue these weapons. For that reason alone, people should be prohibited from possessing extreme weapons. Additionally people exposed to hunting, especially as young children, may become desensitized to the taking of life, which may lead to violence later in life. Unlike movie or video game violence, this violence is real and does involve the taking of actual, as opposed to virtual, life. We should then determine whether hunting as a lifestyle needs to be prohibited as a threat to society.

Children's Toys

It is unlikely that toy guns or other toys precipitate violent or aggressive behavior in children. On the contrary, it may be part of their cognitive and social development. Children learn to control their impulses, delay gratification, think symbolically and view life from another's perspective[36]. All of these are skills that children need to learn in order to operate effectively in society. Most children grow out of that kind of play before their teens. The kind of interaction seen with young children and toy guns is more about domination, heroism, winning and losing than it is about violence.

What is of greater concern is the number of children that have been killed by law enforcement who erroneously believe that the toy gun a child is holding is real. Officers assume that because there are so many firearms in society, a child holding a firearm is armed. That says more about an armed society than it does about children waving toy guns around, and about a society that will use lethal force in almost any situation involving a firearm, real or otherwise.

There is certainly an issue concerning the realism of toy guns. It ought to be clear that these are toys and not real weapons. Mandating certain colors for toy guns and distinctive features setting toy and real guns apart would be helpful.

A society in which a child is suspended from school for pointing a gun-like finger at another child is a society that has become overly neurotic about firearms. The very real deaths that society sees from real firearms spills over into the fantasy world inhabited by children, and probably does them emotional harm. Play ought to be a natural part of a child's development, even rough play. A society in which real firearms are not available at all would have a more realistic view of children at play, and not become hysterical when children act as children. Suspending a child for an innocent action does far more harm than good and sends the message that harmless actions are forbidden.

What is truly repugnant is the arms industry pushing real firearms on small children, as is evident in the Crickett company's products, like its rifle. This is the same .22 rifle that a five-year-old boy used to kill his two-year-old sister. The gun lobby goes further and encourages children to participate in hunting programs. The lesson that this teaches children is that life is of little value, and that killing is a reasonable thing to do.

Conservatives and Gun Disasters

The first instinct of the gun lobby when a gun massacre happens is to find someone to blame. Gun possession, firearm availability, and large capacity magazines are never to blame; it is always something or someone else. Often, the NRA and organizations like it crawl into the woodwork until outrage dissipates, then they emerge screaming about freedom being stripped away by authoritarian government. Seldom do we have a quiet, rational debate over how best to resolve the issues surrounding gun violence. The solution for the gun lobby is always more guns, regardless of the 300 million firearms already in private hands. It is hard to see that providing more guns than the hundreds of millions already out there will change the situation for the better.

Abortion

Former comic Victoria Jackson[1],

"Wasn't the Connecticut killer just doing what abortionists do every day?"

Matt Barber of the Liberty Counsel, concerning the shooting in Aurora, Colorado[2]

"Am I comparing this incredibly wicked, illegal mass murder at Aurora's Century theatre to the incredibly wicked, legal mass murder committed at Planned Parenthoods across the country each day? Absolutely."

Conservative commentators predictably bring out abortion as the proximate cause of almost any disaster. Comparing the slaughter of twenty independently living, breathing, and sentient humans to a blastocyst or embryo demeans the enormous loss of the children of Newtown. A blastocyst, consisting of 70-100 cells, cannot be called human by any reasonable definition any more than a liver or heart is human in its own right. A liver may contain human DNA, but it is no more human than a fetus is independently human. The living infant brain alone can contain anywhere up to 38 billion cells[3], hundreds of millions of times more than a fetus. Once a fetus is viable, and poses no threat to the life of the mother, as ruled by the Supreme Court, it becomes human with incumbent rights. Before that point, it is no more than an integral part of the woman's body.

Even if we were to accept the tragedy of abortion, it still does not alter the brutality of the tragedies in Newtown and Aurora. It is as though conservatives were justifying the brutal acts of Aurora and Newtown because we allow abortion. The two are in no way connected, even in the most convoluted of minds. Conflating the two demonstrates a callous disregard both for the lives lost in the Newtown and Aurora shootings and for the lives of women who need abortions. Women who need abortions are not seen as having human rights any more than the ceaseless victims of gun violence are perceived as having rights. For conservatives, the rights of the gun owner clearly take precedence over the lives of the victims of gun violence and women in difficult situations. By this logic, we may as well legalize all forms of murder, merely because abortion is legal; it is after all, just another way of killing a human.

Mike Huckabee, Fox News commentator had this to say after the shootings in Newtown,

> "Christian owned businesses are told to surrender their values under the edict of government orders to provide tax-funded abortion pills."

There is no government funding of abortion pills, but even if there were, that did not cause Adam Lanza to take so many lives, or to justify the massacre. In a comparison between assault weapons and abortion pills, it is clear what caused the carnage and the broken, dismembered bodies in Sandy Hook. Without an assault weapon and ammunition at his disposal, Lanza would have been hard pressed to cause the massacre. Conservatives like Huckabee need to start taking responsibility for the tens of thousands of unnecessary gun deaths around this nation each year. A little compassion for the victims might go a long way towards advancing his religious agenda.

James Dobson, founder of the conservative Christian group Focus on the Family,

> "We get all up in arms about 20 children being shot in a day care but we don't give one good-glory rip about the 4,000 that were removed violently from the wombs of their mothers in abortion procedures the same day. I believe they use children and Christmas and all that to pull on our heart strings about gun control."

This makes one wonder whether he cares at all about the living, those who have taken their first breath as cognitive, sentient humans. If he professes to favor life over choice, surely the lives of those twenty children had value. That he dismisses their deaths as inconsequential before the Second Amendment is a clear demonstration of his indifference to the living. He claims to care so much about life, yet cares so little about the senseless gun deaths of 36,000 people each year.

There is some evidence to suggest that free access to abortion lowers crime rates in high-risk areas. Unwanted children, or children living in extreme poverty are more likely to become involved in crime, especially violent crime. Crime is often more prevalent in areas with high poverty and high rates of unwanted pregnancy. Whether there is a causal link is certainly debatable, since other researchers point to the waning of the crack cocaine epidemic and the reductions in lead based gasoline as proximate reasons for the reduction in crime.

According to one study[4],

> "Crime began to fall roughly eighteen years after abortion legalization. The five states that allowed abortion in 1970 experienced declines earlier than the rest of

the nation, which legalized in 1973.... Legalized abortion appears to account for as much as 50% of the recent drop in crime"

Sexuality

The Family Research Council has this to say about gun disasters[5],

"If Congress wants to stop these disasters, then it has to address the government's own hostility to the institution of the family and organizations that can address the real problem: the human heart. As I have said before, 'America doesn't need gun control, it needs self-control'. And a Congress that actively discourages it - through abortion, family breakdown, sexual liberalism or religious hostility - is only compounding the problem."

The Council should face up to the fact that the presence of a firearm in the home increases the probability of a member of the household being injured or killed with that firearm. If they were truly concerned about the family, they would demand an end to firearm ownership. Self-control spread through a population is just not sufficient as a deterrent to gun violence, any more than it is for any crime.

Mike Huckabee, inimitable Fox News commentator,

"We dismiss the notion of natural law and the notion that there are moral absolutes and seemed amazed when some kids make it their own morality to kill innocent children."

Huckabee does not produce any credible evidence that Lanza, the Newtown killer, was influenced by an absence of moral absolutes or had any concept of natural law. Lanza's mother was a survivalist who preferred collecting extreme weapons and home schooling her child, which by Huckabee's own admission should have shielded him from the influences of public schools. Millions of school children pass through public schools unscathed and do not perpetrate acts of violence against anyone including schoolmates.

One is left to wonder whether his mother's own delusions about a decaying society, as demonstrated by her survivalist inclinations, were the proximate cause of his psychotic break. It may well be that her anti-social disposition created an overly active sense of paranoia in him towards society in general and the public school system in particular, which led to the massacre. Either way, it is speculation as to the proximate cause of the massacre.

Evolution

Rick Warren, Evangelical minister and senior pastor of the Saddleback Church claimed,

> "When students are taught they are no different from animals, they act like it."

Pastor Sam Morris of the Old Paths Baptist Church in Tennessee,

> "Its the teaching of evolution and how to be a homo in public schools. Abortion is
> a far worse problem."

Precisely how the teaching of scientifically accepted fact induces anyone to commit atrocities is unclear. No doubt, the same was said after Copernicus claimed that the Earth revolves around the Sun and rotates on its own axis in defiance of Biblical inerrancy. Perhaps the principles of General Relativity and the eradication of Aristotelian observations caused the Holocaust or other natural or human disasters.

If conservative religious leaders understood the principles of evolutionary biology, they may find that homosexuality is a rational part of life. Life does not fit neatly into a box; basic evolutionary processes produce an almost infinite variety of life. Ultimately, success or failure in life is certainly partly enhanced by the ability to reproduce or not. Those individuals within a species who are able to reproduce pass their genes on to another generation, those who are unable to, do not.

Speciation, genetic drift, adaptive radiation and mutation may ultimately result in members of a species that are unable to reproduce for one reason or another. The results of evolutionary processes are neither moral nor immoral they are morally neutral. Teaching about evolution no more results in gun massacres or gun violence than does the teaching of atomic theory, continental drift theory, theoretical mathematics or universal gravitation.

Criminals Carry Out Mass Shootings

An article by the New York Times, in which they studied 100 mass killings, stated that many mass killers were anything but criminals. Most criminals try to get away with their crimes by running from the law. Regular homicides are notoriously difficult to solve, with almost a third remaining unsolved[6]. Of the 102 killers profiled by the Times, eighty-nine did not attempt to get away from the scene of the massacre. None of the rest got away. These are clearly not normal criminals.

Otherwise normal people carry out most mass shootings. Just like the rest of the population, many shooters have mental problems, but not all were criminals before their mass killing. They become criminals once they committed their atrocity, not before. Millions of people have mental problems, but most do not commit crimes. The mere fact that there are so many people with mental problems makes those people a normal part of society.

Gun advocates claim that criminals commit gun crimes, but a person is only a criminal once they have committed a criminal act. Technically speaking once someone commits a crime he or she ay be considered a criminal, but in the eyes of the law they are only considered a criminal once tried and convicted. They may be accused of committing a crime, but they are not yet criminals under the law, unless they have prior records. Thus, perfectly ordinary people commit crimes, even mass killers or spree killers.

There are many people walking around that have not yet committed a crime, but may do so in the future. That in and of itself does not make them criminals, even if they think dark thoughts or plan to commit a crime. At least not until thought becomes a crime, and we head down the dark road portrayed by George Orwell in 1984. Even the planning of a crime does not become a crime until one takes concrete actions to commit that crime. Even then, if they change their mind and abort their actions, they are not criminals. Once someone has committed a crime, it may be a criminal act, but he or she is not a criminal under law until they have been tried and convicted of that crime.

Clearly once a person start to commit mass murder, they have committed a criminal act, but until they are found guilty they are not strictly speaking criminals. To say otherwise is to imply the existence of a criminal class who are guilty even before they have committed an offense. Such thinking is discriminatory and serves only to marginalize certain people based on race, ethnicity or social status.

In Texas, State Sen. Glenn Hegar sponsored legislation giving Texans the right to keep concealed weapons in their cars while parked on company property says,

> "We have to very clearly look at the difference between citizens who are following the law and those who are criminals who want to commit terrible crimes."

A great many people who are not criminals commit terrible crimes. If they have not yet been convicted of a crime, they cannot legally be considered criminals. If you were to say that anyone who commits a crime and is convicted is a criminal, absolutely true, but not until they have actually committed the crime and been convicted. If they had no criminal conviction before the crime, a criminal did not commit the crime.

You cannot tell whether a person is a criminal before they commit a criminal act, any more than you can divine anything about a person until they have performed some concrete action. They may have a propensity to commit a given action, and may never act on that propensity. It is rather like having a talent, you may use that talent, or you may allow it to become dormant. Using their logic, I am variously a concert pianist, guitar aficionado, brilliant scientist and a great many other things. For conservatives to say that a criminal class commits crimes is a logical fallacy. Under American law, any person is extended the right to be innocent until found guilty by a court.

Many people diligently follow the law until some point in their lives, and then break it. Up until that point, they are not criminals. It is easy for conservatives and the gun lobby to say that criminals break the law because it sounds correct, and it is, but only after conviction. At that point it is pointless to talk about criminals breaking the law because by definition, someone convicted of a crime is a criminal and has broken the law.

Criminals are far more likely to be the victims of firearms than they are to commit mass shootings. In Washington DC, a study of detainees found that 1 in 4 had been wounded in events unrelated to their incarceration[7]. 83% witnessed someone being shot, 46% had a family member killed by a gun. These criminals report being shot by other criminals, not law abiding citizens.

Restrictive Gun laws Don't Stop Criminals

According to ALEC, "the National Institute of Justice has determined that restrictive gun laws are ineffective against violent criminals who show contempt for all laws"[8]. The fact of the matter is that if criminals are unable to get guns freely in society, they will have no choice but to find them elsewhere, which they may do, but for the majority of criminals, obtaining those guns will be financially untenable and logistically impossible.

That alone will reduce the gun violence in society. This happens in most countries across the developed world. Gun violence is extremely low in those countries, the sole exception being the United States, which has guns freely available on the street and in supermarkets like Wal-Mart.

Those of criminal intent will commit crimes, regardless of the laws we put in place, at least as far as the gun lobby is concerned. That does not stop us from having laws against rape, murder, robbery or fraud, all of which reduce crime. We put laws in place to restrain the law-abiding citizenry from breaking those laws. Most people will obey those laws if they are in place. If they are not, there is no reason for people to act in accordance with moral or ethical standards.

If we were to follow ALEC logic, we would have no laws at all, which of course would suit them down to the ground. This is why we implement laws, to show people what the penalty for breaking those laws might be, and preventing most sensible people from breaking them.

As for the National Institute of Justice, I can find no evidence suggesting that they believe that gun restrictions are ineffective. On the contrary, what they say is that there are insufficient data available for them to make a determination. They "support the development and maintenance of the National Violent Death Reporting System and the National Incident Based Reporting System, both of which would provide comprehensive data on violent deaths and crime, a small part of which is data on firearm use[9]". The gun lobby has steadfastly opposed such efforts because of the fear of what they may discover.

Opponents of anti-gun-violence laws claim that it is difficult to keep high-risk individuals from acquiring weapons even under federal enforcement, just as it was to stop the sale and use of liquor during Prohibition. It is often difficult to stop people from indulging in criminal behavior, but that does not stop us from empowering law enforcement to compel people to obey the laws. We do not give up because people disobey the law; we endure despite the difficulties.

If some individuals give up some of their rights in order for society to safe from harm, that is the price to be paid for living in a sophisticated, modern society. We try to police that society to the best of our ability, without infringing on basic rights, which do not include the ownership of destructive weapons.

The more difficult it becomes to obtain extreme weapons, the less likely criminals or anyone else is likely to use them on vulnerable populations. Fewer extreme weapons available legally will push up the cost to own these weapons. When the cost to obtain any product rises, simple economics dictates that fewer people are able to obtain that product. With fewer extreme weapons in peoples homes and available through gun dealers, fewer will end up on the street and fewer will be used in gun crimes. This is the simple logic of supply and demand, unless the gun lobby has revoked economic law. As it is, purchasing weapons on a black market is going to be more costly and more dangerous. With availability on legal markets curtailed, it will push prices higher on black markets, and probably exceed the ability of criminals to pay.

More Guns Make Us Safer

The United States has the highest rate of gun ownership in the world and the second highest rate of gun deaths among industrialized nations[10]. In all industrialized nations, the higher the rate of gun ownership, the higher the death rate by guns. The only exception to this rule was Mexico, which has a higher death rate than the United States and fewer guns. That country is currently enmeshed in a low-level drug war fueled by guns trafficked in from the United States.

The rankings of Finland and Switzerland, which are quite high, are due mostly to suicides rather than homicides. When corrected for suicides, the United States leads the industrialized world by miles in gun homicides and number of guns owned.

Higher firearm numbers lead to more unintentional, nonfatal firearm related injuries. Between June 1992 and May 1994, 34,485 people were treated for these injuries in US emergency departments. The majority of the patients were male (87%) aged 15 to 34 years (61%). 38% required hospitalization. Most injuries were to an extremity (73%), self-inflicted (70%), involved a handgun (57%) and occurred during common gun related activities[11]. The higher number of firearms did not make people safer and only led to higher numbers of injuries.

In Brazil between 2003 and 2004, firearm deaths in Brazil dropped 8% subsequent to a statutory gun buy-back program[12]. More than 200,000 firearms were turned in within three months. By mid 2005, the number doubled. In Colombia, arms control programs reduced gun violence by 11% between 1994 and 2002, including cities like Bogotá and Medellín[13]. The firearm homicide rate almost halved, falling from 46 in 1998 to 27 in 2010. In Bogotá, the mayor imposed a citywide ban on carrying firearms in public; the murder rate fell to its lowest in 27 years[14]. The rate is now 16.1 compared to 22 before the ban. This was achieved in two countries with some of the world's highest gun homicide rates.

In the mass shootings that plague the United States on a regular basis, and recently look as though they are becoming an epidemic, no armed civilian has managed to stop a single incident. In other incidents, armed civilians have been either severely injured or killed, without stopping the shooter.

Studies have shown that in a live shooter situation, lets say a classroom; armed students consistently fail to stop the shooter or prevent their own deaths. They were also more likely to shoot potential victims than the shooter. Even well trained professionals have difficulty succeeding in chaotic situations, such as that in a darkened theater like Aurora. Training for these situations needs to be continuous and ongoing and relying on untrained civilians is likely to lead to more deaths. Even law enforcement officers react to crises in unpredictable ways, often exacerbating a situation rather than resolving it.

Despite the rapidly increasing number of guns in America, mass shootings have actually increased, not decreased as predicted by the gun industry and its lobbyists. During President Obama's tenure, gun ownership has risen at a dramatic pace, yet the rate of mass shootings has increased during this time, not decreased[15]. Between 1995 and 2012, the number of guns in private hands in this country has increased from an estimated 200m to more than 310m, or more than 50%, while the population grew only 20%. This indicates that the number of guns per person has also increased rapidly.

Clearly there is a relationship between the number of guns in the population and the number of massacres of civilians using these weapons. Of the 62 massacres since 1982, 25 have occurred in the last six years. The average per year before that time was two massacres. Since 2006, the average has doubled. This is during the greatest private firearm buildup in American history. If the logic of the gun lobby had any credibility, mass shootings should have fallen in number. In 2012, there were seven mass shootings, with the death toll exceeding 140 people, and many more injured.

Handguns account for about a third of all firearms owned in the United States[16], while one third of households own firearms. Of households with firearms, 61% are estimated to have at least one handgun[17]. Handguns are used in half of all homicides[18], 70% of firearm homicides and 70% of all firearm suicides. Handguns account for 77% of all traced guns used in crime[19].

Semi-automatic pistols cause appreciably more serious wounds per weapon than revolvers or long guns, possibly due to their greater magazine capacity[20]. Due to their ability to deliver a higher rate of fire in a shorter period[21], semi-automatic and automatic weapons are able to inflict greater injury, causing an increased number of bullet wounds per incident per body and thus higher mortality[22,23]. In a comparison of revolvers to pistols, pistols caused a 15% increase in wounded victims over revolvers. Pistols are generally favored over revolvers, possibly due to their greater capacity. Where a revolver generally holds 5-6 cartridges, a pistol can hold seven rounds or more.

African Americans are far more likely to be the victims of firearm homicide than whites. The homicide rate among black males (30.3) was 8 times that of white males (3.7) in 2007[24].

The gun industry would have us believe that greater numbers of people are purchasing firearms than ever before. This is not the case; in fact, fewer people are buying a greater number of firearms. Gun owners in the United States, which comprises only 1% of the world's population, own as many as one third of all guns worldwide[25]. This trend is worrying, since those increasingly well-armed individuals pose an accelerating threat to the security of the United States.

A survey published in the Injury Prevention Journal, determined that 20% of gun owners with the greatest number of firearms possessed about 65% of the nations' guns[26]. It also found that men are far more likely than are women to own firearms, despite the fact that women are a more vulnerable population. The General Social Survey found that only 1 in 10 women own firearms. The general decline in gun homicides coincides with fewer gun owners, despite the increase in the number of firearms.

Contrary to popular belief, armed civilians do not stop mass shooters, despite the large numbers of firearms in the U.S. In those states with Right-To-Carry laws, aggravated assaults show a distinct rise in comparison to those states not adopting these laws[27]. Firearms claim the lives of more children than any cause other than motor vehicle accidents[28]. In Australia, gun restrictions reduced gun massacres from 13 over 18 years to zero in the following decade. In "Shall Issue" states, firearms must be sold to people, and studies find that crime rises after the introduction of these laws[29]. These and other facts show that the presence of firearms fuels gun violence, death and injury, and gun regulation does what it is supposed to do, reduce deaths.

The presence of firearms may actually act as a stimulus to the commission of crimes, including burglary and theft partly because of the ease with which firearms may be sold. The other danger is that as civilians arm themselves, effectively neutralizing any advantage that one armed person has over another armed person, there will be pressure on people to purchase more efficient, effective or extreme firearms; an arms race, which only costs more in economic terms and in terms of lives lost.

Gun owners who possess firearms in the belief that the weapons can be used in self-defense are operating under a false set of assumptions. Firearms are 22 times more likely to be used in criminal assault, homicide, suicide or accidental death than for self-defense[30]. By that token, gun owners are far safer not having firearms in the home, since having a firearm is correlated with a far higher rate of violence than self-defense. It is irrational to continue to possess extreme weapons in the face of the evidence against possession. Guns as sold in the United States do far more damage to society than they allegedly prevent.

Civilians Can Stop Violence

Civilians are not trained in hostile fire situations, and many do not even have the rudiments of training necessary to successfully control their weapons. During police interventions, trained law enforcement officers often make mistakes, with killings of unarmed civilians all too common. Despite their training, law enforcement officers are often incapable of stopping bloodshed. In an incident in New York City, for instance, police officers confronted a gunman and wounded nine civilians in the process[31].

Civilians are more likely to increase the violence in shootings than to assist in preventing gun violence. Dr. Stephen Hargarten, Medical College of Wisconsin says, "Civilian shooters are less likely to hit their targets than police in these circumstances. [32]" He also says that mass shootings need to be seen as a public health emergency to ensure that policy makers can better concentrate on controlling the violence epidemic. He says that if we had an outbreak of Ebola, the nations foremost experts would be attempting to solve it, which they have manifestly failed to do with the firearm violence epidemic.

The ability to react successfully in live shooter situations is a product of intensive and ongoing training. Like any other skill, it is quickly lost over time, and even professionals have to train continuously in order to be effective, which is why law enforcement agencies insist on range training. Expecting an armed, untrained civilian to react correctly, especially in a confused situation, where armed assailants are not easily identified is a recipe for disaster, and a greater number of innocent people are likely to be killed than might otherwise be the case.

Developed nations rely on their law enforcement agencies to provide security for their citizens. When greater numbers of civilians possess armaments, it becomes increasingly difficult for those agencies to ensure uniform security for its population. Increases in guns are likely to lead to armed violence, banditry and organized crime, which in turn is likely to increase demand for weapons[33]. We should not be relying on civilians to provide us with safety and security, or expecting individuals to provide that security for themselves. For a variety of reasons, people are unable to defend themselves and have a right to demand that their societies provide that security.

Whether an individual decides to carry and use a firearm depends on the consequences of that decision[34]. In those nations where the legal consequences of carrying or using a firearm are particularly severe, the firearm death and injury rate is invariably far lower than in those nations with irresponsible laws. The comparison between Japan and the United States is particularly salient. In Japan, carrying or using a firearm is dealt with swiftly, resulting in an extremely low firearm crime rate, whereas in the United States, Concealed Carry laws and Stand Your Ground laws lower the bar on homicide, leading to far higher death rates.

In those cases in which an armed civilian appears to have prevented a shooting, most of the shooters had already completed their rampage and were either out of ammunition, reloading, or running from the scene. What is startling, considering the 300 million guns in private hands in the United States is how few rampage shootings are halted or prevented by armed civilians. In other incidents, armed civilians who have attempted to intervene have been shot or injured.

Retired or off-duty law enforcement officers, who are trained to react to such situations, have managed to halt some shootings[35]. Often, people who stop mass shooters are themselves not armed. Jared Loughner, the Tucson shooter who shot Rep. Gabrielle Giffords and killed a nine-year-old girl, was subdued when he stopped to reload. Some shooters have been stopped when a car was rammed into their vehicle. One investigation found that armed civilians stop only 1.6% of mass shootings[36]. Even in the single case in which this happened, the perpetrator was pursued after the incident and killed. By this measure, none of the 62 mass shootings in the past 30 years have been stopped by an armed civilian[37].

It is odd that despite the 300 million guns in this country, the 8 million concealed weapons permits, and the 34% of people that are armed, no one manages to stop massacres. Surely, there was a single, armed civilian that could have stopped at least one massacre. Clearly, then, they did not. The sheer probability indicates that someone ought to have stopped at least one, and yet the sad reality is that no one did. That on its own argues strongly against the misguided belief that "good guy" stop "bad guys".

The Evil in People

The idea that a killer like Adam Lanza acted because he was evil is another way to misdirect and mislead the anti-gun-violence debate. It implies that people are not acting of their own accord, but through possession by supernatural forces beyond their control, or through innate sinfulness. Instead of introducing legislation or regulations that circumscribe people's actions and lay down remedies, punishments or inducements to reduce violence, certain religious adherents believe that we should change our morals.

This is the same incoherent argument used when talking about mental health issues, that because violence is innate or because people are sinners, nothing useful can be done to prevent gun violence. This continues the idea that man is not in control of his own destiny, that he cannot manipulate his own environment. This argument proposes that only when we identify all those with mental health issues, or those that are evil, can we tackle society's problems. Laying the blame on a violent and sin-sick world does nothing to tackle the very real problem of gun violence.

Franklin Graham, president of the Billy Graham Evangelistic Association claims[38],

> "Moral heartfelt transformation is really the only solution to the deadly and dangerous ills that are plaguing our nation. The Scripture says we need a new heart, not new legislation or regulations...In this violent, sin-sick world, our only hope is the Prince of Peace."

By this token, we should stop producing any and all legislation, do nothing constructive to tackle our problems and spend our lives praying. Democratic society would cease to function at all if it stopped acting as referee in resolving society's ills. Some claim aware that the solution lies in identifying those most likely to do violence, yet the gun lobby, the gun industry and the evangelical church are not pushing harder for background checks. It is the single most effective way to keep firearms from people who are not competent to use them.

The use of the purported evil inherent in people to excuse the possession of extreme firearms, amounts to an abolishing of the duty of the church. Any church founded on Christian principles must have as its foundation the sanctity of life. By opposing sensible gun restrictions and using preposterous, disjointed and inchoate arguments about sin and evil, some religious organizations are allowing for the perpetuation of unnecessary deaths and injuries around the country. No biblical reference promotes the possession of extreme firearms; on the contrary, the message of Christ is one of peace, not one of violence.

Greg Stier, founder of Dare 2 Share Ministries had this to say[39],

"What happened at Sandy Hook Elementary School was at a level of malevolence beyond any earthly explanation or solution. Like a river of magma underneath the earths crust, unimaginable evil burst forth that day, looking for a place to explode."

The fact of the matter is that we do not know why Lanza did what he did, but to claim that there is no explanation is to renounce the use of reason entirely. Society can and does explain gun massacres, and it can endeavor to explain and resolve the problem of gun violence. Organizations like this use religion to justify the possession of extreme weapons rather than attempt to prevent violence, which after all is part of their *raison d'etre*.

Connecticut Governor Dan Malloy[40],

"Evil visited this community today and it is too early to speak of recovery ... we will do whatever we can to overcome this event, we will get through it."

It was not evil that visited the community, it was a young man, whether disturbed or not we will probably never determine, but he was armed with legally purchased extreme weapons that destroyed the lives of so many. It does not help to say that we will get through the disaster, what helps is to decide what we can do to stop people from getting extreme weapons and using them on vulnerable populations. We can pray for rain all we like, but it is only when we go out and plant crops and build irrigation ditches, that we will receive a harvest. The prayers make us feel good, but planting and irrigating addresses the problem.

Wayne LaPierre had this to say after Sandy Hook,

"More guns, you will claim, are the NRA's answer to everything! Your implication will be that guns are evil and have no place in society, much less in our schools. But since when did "gun" automatically become a bad word."

The gun lobby does indeed posit guns as the answer to every disaster, every massacre, and all the gun violence in the U.S. It is not that guns are inherently evil, but the intention behind designing, manufacturing, producing, selling and using them may well be. A sane, peaceful society has no need for firearms, or weapons of any kind. We need to ask why any sane, sensible person finds a need for an assault weapon, for large capacity magazines, for fragmenting bullets, silencers, laser sights or armor piercing ammunition, unless it is to harm others or take life. Gun is most definitely a bad word; little good ever came from the barrel of a gun; lives are still lost, whether human or otherwise.

In an optimistic survey of evangelical Christian leaders, at least 73% agreed on the need for stricter gun regulation[41]. Given their penetration in areas of the country with high levels of gun possession, they have an obligation to press their congregants to support stricter gun regulations. That they have not done so is an indictment of their ideology.

Using the evil in men to excuse gun violence is a surrender of our ability to handle difficult and seemingly intractable problems. The idea that we should give up in the face of adversity is inimical to the spirit of the Republic and the hardship faced at its founding.

The Mass Media

Conservatives and gun rights activists often blame the media for gun violence. Some debate has grown up around the role that the mass media play in mass shootings, with the implication that any coverage of the events can induce others to perpetrate similar crimes.

The problem here is to draw a relationship between two things based on the data. As the gun industry enjoys pointing out, correlation does not imply causation. We can say that when a person buys a gun, he does not have to use it to perpetrate an act of violence, but having the gun does make it easier to do so. The fact that the news media promote coverage of an event like a massacre does not make people go out and commit mass murder, and it makes it no easier to do so. Someone intent on mass murder may continue with his plans regardless of what the media say or do. How well he manages to do so depends on the means available to him.

The idea that mass media cause events to happen is tenuous at best. The media cover many events that do not cause similar incidents, like war, assault, battery, car accidents or political wrangling. Some may use the media to get attention; politicians often do or say outrageous things to get attention. Some mass killers might want publicity, but many of them kill themselves, which indicates that the publicity does not mean much to them.

Someone who is planning to commit an atrocity may be incited by a newspaper or magazine article, or may just use a library or bookstore to research mass killings. The proximate cause is quite likely to be something else, a divorce, unemployment, or the break up of a relationship. It would be hard to say that articles or coverage of a similar event caused a killer to commit a crime.

The gun lobby blames movies, unarmed schools, the mentally ill or video games, yet completely discount its responsibility for mass killings. Without the extreme weapons that the gun lobby imposes on society, and which were used in Newtown to slaughter twenty children and their teachers, killers would find it difficult to carry out massacres. To put it in terms the gun lobby can understand, newspapers and movies do not kill people; people with extreme weapons kill people.

Wayne LaPierre, NRA chief,

"Rather than face their own moral failings, the media demonize lawful gun owners."

The fact is people with guns commit gun crimes. It is difficult to commit a gun crime without possessing a firearm. The gun owner is still at fault whether that firearm is stolen from him or used by him. When gun owners become more responsible and insist on tighter gun regulations, the media can stop demonizing them. The media report the news, that is their responsibility, and they ask tough questions such as, who is to blame, how can we prevent crime from happening, and who is accountable. They are the true guardians of our freedoms, not gun owners with extreme weapons.

Good Guys with Guns

The gun lobby declares, "Good guys with guns are the only defense against bad guys with guns". Yet, the Second Amendment, as interpreted by the gun lobby, is the most effective way for "bad guys", criminals, drug lords, psychopaths and other people bent on mischief to obtain firearms. We do not know the intentions of people who buy guns, and there is as much chance of reasonable people buying guns as unreasonable people. With extreme weapons, it is more likely that unreasonable people will want to buy them, which changes the balance of force between reasonable and unreasonable people.

The question we need to ask is whether those people buying guns are more or less likely to be rational, reasonable people. People intent on harming others, or those who are delusional or conspiracy minded are probably more likely to buy firearms than are people that have a rational perspective towards their government and others. Conservatives are more likely to own firearms, and more likely to mistrust government, foreigners, and those who differ from them.

During a training session in which a shooter enters a school, State Senator Jeremy Hutchinson (R-TX) accidentally shot a teacher with a rubber bullet instead of the presumed killer, demonstrating clearly what can go wrong in any shooting[42]. The alleged 'good guy' with a gun shot another 'good guy' with a gun. In a real shooting, the situation is not controlled as it is in a training exercise, it is dynamic, fluid and chaotic and it is difficult to tell who the shooter is. When civilians are armed, it is impossible for law enforcement to tell who the perpetrator is, and armed civilians or innocent people can die.

Jeremy Hutchinson[43],

> "The tough part is when law enforcement does arrive, it's hard to distinguish between the good guys with guns and the bad guys with guns. There were gun shots in the hallway, there's a man shooting into the classroom, and I shot that person (with a simulation bullet)"

In a live fire situation, if civilians were armed, there could be one or more shooters, a dozen armed teachers and security officers involved. Add in a few dozen police officers, and the chance of an even greater disaster rises dramatically. Bullets could be flying in all directions, and with a school filled with young children who could be panicked, screaming and running in all directions, a lot more people could die before the tragedy is over, including teachers, students, police officers or other first responders.

Prospective killers do not announce that they will be entering a public space at a particular time, or what they will be wearing, what they look like and what weapons they will be carrying. Even well trained law enforcement officers have a difficult time distinguishing perpetrators from civilians. Killers do not wear uniforms, black hats, bandanas or eye patches; they are likely to look like any member of the public. When everyone is armed, an armed civilian cannot know whom to shoot. In a chaotic, panicked situation, even a can of iced tea can look like a weapon.

Law enforcement officers need to spend a great deal of time on gun ranges practicing for armed shooter events and to keep their skills finely honed. Armed civilians do not have the time to spend on keeping trained, which is why we pay law enforcement to ensure our safety, not civilians. All we need as a society is an untrained armed civilian vigilante creating havoc during a shooting. There is no way to determine whether we can trust untrained, armed civilians with our lives, or those of our children.

Having armed civilians in a shooting situation makes the job of law enforcement even more difficult. There is no way for them to tell who the killer is, and they must assume that anyone with a firearm is a shooter. During the Tucson massacre initiated by Jared Loughner, an armed civilian came close to shooting an innocent civilian after mistaking that person for the killer. The man holding the gun had just taken it away from the real killer and was holding it when the newly arrived armed civilian saw him and ordered him to drop the weapon. It could well have ended badly for either of them. It could also have become a firefight between armed civilians in which even more people died. The gun lobby uses this as an example of a good guy with a gun, but the reality is far from the fantasy they portray. Massacres do not happen in nice neat packages.

Even well trained law enforcement agents do not barge into a live shooter situation, especially with live hostages. It takes specially trained operatives to deal with these situations, and teachers, security guards and janitors in schools do not have this specialized training. Even Presidents, surrounded by armed guards have fallen prey to would-be assassins[44]. One of the nations top snipers and a friend, both armed, were killed on a gun range, by a 'bad guy' with a gun[45]. In a standoff with an armed intruder, a New York Police Officer accidentally killed Andrea Rebello, a student at Hofstra University[46]. This is another example of a trained, law enforcement officer killing a bystander during the commission of a violent crime.

Society does not need armed vigilantes on the streets; we need well-trained law enforcement officers, preferably without firearms, as in the United Kingdom, who respect the members of a community and work to keep guns and crime off the streets. We do not need a gun owner who believes he is the reincarnation of John Wayne or Dirty Harry waving his firearm around in public. Society has a right to be safe from people claiming to be 'good guys'.

Wayne LaPierre had this to say after the Boston Marathon bombing[47],

Residents were imprisoned behind the locked doors of their homes - a terrorist with bombs and guns outside. Frightened citizens, sheltered in place, with no means to defend themselves or their families from whatever may come crashing through the door"

Imagine a city of armed civilians, sitting in their homes waiting with loaded firearms. The slightest movement outside may cause some of them to react and shoot innocent pedestrians, a man whose car broke down and needs to contact a repair shop, someone sitting on the sidewalk, a woman talking on a cell phone, or a son coming home to surprise his parents. All society needs in a lockdown is a city of armed, paranoid residents waiting to shoot someone. If society was not armed, the Boston Marathon Bomber may have been caught a lot sooner; instead, being armed, there was the inevitable firefight when he was found.

The gun lobby has managed to create a war zone, in which everyone is seen as a possible threat, and everyone is armed, a society in which any perceived slight can end in death. This is not a safe society, or a healthy society; neurosis is not healthy for any nation. More guns in a massacre will ultimately end with more deaths. We should not want to put our lives in the hands of untrained civilians.

When a person walks into a restaurant, shopping mall or other public space, and he clearly carries a concealed weapon, society has not way to trust that his intentions are honorable. Society cannot gauge whether this person is not intent on harming others with his weapon. We as unarmed civilians have no way to believe that he is a good guy. Rather, we should instead be terrified of anyone carrying a firearm because the probability is far greater that we will be harmed than helped. It is quite credible that the bad guy with a gun stops the good guy with a gun, as has happened during massacres. Someone who used to be a good guy can easily turn his gun on his wife and children. Is a five year old that shoots his two-year-old sister with a rifle a good guy or a bad guy? Life is not a Hollywood movie set; the person intent on doing harm to others is more committed to violence than someone trying to stop him. The "bad guy" is more likely to use the weapon than is the "good guy". Good guys generally do not turn to violence to resolve complex issues.

Despite claims that good guys with guns stop bad guys with guns, people do not fit neatly into one category or the other. People with ostensibly honorable intentions towards firearm ownership may commit gun crimes under certain circumstances, or use their firearms when it is not warranted. There is no simple way to determine whether someone is likely to be a good guy or a bad guy, and like most aspects of social life, people fall along a continuum, from people who are highly unlikely to use a firearm under almost any circumstance, to those willing to use firearms in any circumstance whether warranted or not. Even then, people may move along that continuum depending on circumstance and changing beliefs. People may also be at different points on that continuum depending on the situation.

According to LaPierre,

"The only thing that stops a bad guy with a gun is a good guy with a gun."

Of all his statements, this one is perhaps the most disingenuous and juvenile. Firstly, during massacres, what normally stops the shooter is that he runs out of ammunition - if we insisted on smaller magazines, the shooting would stop a lot earlier. In many instances in which a member of the public has tried to stop a shooting, the killer shoots the member of the public, including shooting at and killing law enforcement officers.

Secondly, when a prospective gun owner walks into a gun shop or gun show, we have no way of knowing whether this person is a "good guy" or someone intent on causing maximum casualties during a shooting rampage. Since the gun lobby does not allow for reasonable background checks, the seller is not compelled to perform one. This means that anyone with criminal intent is able to legally buy a gun and as much ammunition as he pleases, because the gun lobby has forced society to adhere to a legal perversion of the Second Amendment. Someone that buys a gun is not automatically a "good guy", which is why sensible countries have intensive background checks and restrictions on what a person may purchase.

Cultural differences cause lower gun death rates

Some in the pro gun lobby argue that the reason that some societies have lower gun death rates is due to multiple cultural differences between societies. Those societies with low death rates from guns do indeed share certain characteristics, none of which has a cultural bias.

Firstly, those societies introduce strict gun regulation. Weapons are restricted to handguns or rifles. Extensive background checks, fingerprinting, investigating references, questioning the purpose of owning the weapon, and waiting periods are all part of the laws of those societies. If that is a cultural difference, then yes, this society is different, in that it has no comprehensive anti-gun-violence system in place.

Societies with higher death rates that subsequently institute and enforce gun restrictions experience a decline in the number of deaths over time. Countries that experience gun massacres and subsequently introduce gun regulations experience the same decline in the death rate from all causes. The culture of those nations does not change after the introduction of gun regulations, but the laws do change, and that plainly is what causes the drop in deaths.

There is no substantial cultural difference between the United States and the United Kingdom. We share the same heritage, speak the same language for the most part, and share certain aspects of the law and philosophical background. The population of both countries has a similar composition, including people from many nations around the world. Yet, the United States has the highest death rate by gun in the developed world, and the United Kingdom one of the lowest.

The United States and Australia probably have more in common than any other English-speaking nation on Earth, with the possible exception of Canada, with which the U.S. shares an extremely long border and centuries of common history. Australia has a similar heritage of gun owning and an untamed frontier, and yet they have managed to control gun violence to the point that it is many times lower than that in the U.S. Canada, similarly, which has a high rate of gun ownership, has low rates of gun violence and low rates of gun homicide.

Income inequality and a deteriorating social safety net are some differences between the U.S. and other nations that may play a part in gun violence in addition to inconsiderate or non-existent gun laws. Continuing conservative attacks on the Middle Class, unions, education and a lack of economic fairness may spur greater gun violence, and possibly the need to own extreme weapons. If government is seen as not caring for the needs of the people, it may create resentment and a fear of government.

The only cultural difference between these nations is that the U.S. refuses to introduce common sense gun restrictions. The U.S. also insists that guns can be used in self-defense despite evidence that guns in the home are more likely to be used on inhabitants of those homes than on intruders. The argument that the U.S. has a cultural affinity for firearms is entirely circular, since we know that higher gun ownership rates on average, controlling for other societal aspects, lead to higher rates of death by firearm.

Anatomy of Massacres

Overview

Since 1982, there have been 62 mass murders in the United States. Of the weapons used in these tragedies, almost 80%, representing 49 of the killers, were obtained legally[1]. Semi-automatic handguns with high capacity magazines were by far the most popular weapons of choice, followed by assault rifles[2]. Twenty-five of these incidents have occurred since 2006, seven in 2012 alone.

More than half of these incidents were either workplace (20) or school (12) shootings. The rest were in shopping malls, restaurants, religious and government buildings. Forty-four of the killers were white men, with only one woman involved. The average age of the killers was 35, with one being 11 years old[3]. While the absolute number of homicides each year appears to be decreasing, the number of mass shootings is rising. Of the 12 most deadly shootings in American history, six have occurred since 2007[4].

Assault weapons or high capacity magazines were used in 12 of 56 mass shootings analyzed by Mayors against Illegal Guns. These weapons injured 135% more people than in other shootings and caused 57% more deaths than in other shootings[5]. In 57% of cases, the shooter killed a current or former spouse, intimate partner or family member. The use of assault weapons clearly causes a greater number of injuries and death than other firearms.

Despite the blame placed on mental health as the proximate cause of mass shootings, only four of the 56 killers had been called to the attention of medical, school or legal authorities[6]. Only 13 of the 56 shootings took place in gun free zones, while 32 occurred entirely within private residences[7].

Massacres in America are becoming more deadly, and close together. The number of massacres is increasing, and the death toll keeps rising. Congress, and even the American people appear apathetic about the fatalities and injuries, unable to take even the simplest actions to change the dynamic. Gun restrictions that other nations find common sense are routinely ignored or explained away.

And people continue to die.

Who Commits Massacres

A study completed by the New York Times concerning 100 rampage attacks is illuminating. According to the article, the killers had much in common; they were not high on drugs or inebriated; they were not racists or Satanists; they were not addicted to violent video games, movies or music. Most are white men, but a few were women, Asian or black. Many were college educated, but mostly unemployed. Many were military veterans. The weapons they carried were semi-automatic, for the most part easily and legally obtained. Often they tell others about their plans. Many do not try to escape, and often commit suicide. In these sprees, 425 people died and 510 were injured. Half of the killers showed signs of serious mental health problems[8].

While around 60% of the killers showed an interest in violent video games, movies or television, there is little evidence that this created the rampage. The racial composition of the killers reflects population demographics to some extent. Only six of the killers were women, all of whom displayed the disturbed, aggressive attitudes of the males. Killers were more likely to have a military background and were generally older than other killers, with more in their 40's and 50's. Of those killers over 25, all but nine had at least some college education. The mix between massacres committed in rural and urban areas is similar.

Some editorials have targeted white men as the most likely to perpetrate these killings[9], but evidence from mass killings around the world show that the propensity for these events is spread among various ethnic groups. Massacres occur in nations like Uganda, Yemen, South Africa, Columbia, Brazil, China and India[10]. Nidal Malik Hasan, born of Palestinian parents, for instance, committed the Fort Hood shooting[11]. The distinction is that the United States has more than its fair share of gun violence and that its rate of gun violence is far higher than any other developed nation. Massacres in the U.S. are far more likely to be perpetrated by firearms than any other weapon.

Why No-one Stops Them

It is likely that white men perpetrate these horrors because a greater proportion of white men have access to these weapons, and are encouraged to become involved in the firearm community. It is also likely that white men lead the fight against gun rights because more of their support emanates from the gun industry and other white men, who are more likely to be involved in the gun community. White men are more likely to *"buy, sell and manufacture guns for profit and attend gun shows[12]"*, because they have the financial means, and because they are encouraged to participate in the gun community, including hunting and gun 'sport'.

Another questionable explanation was that all personnel at the Newtown school were women, and that there were no men present to stop the shooter[13]. Since none of the mass shootings since 1982 have been stopped by a man, or by an armed man, or by anyone else, this explanation is thin at best. Some clearly still believe in the myth of masculinity preventing violence, a naive belief bred of too many Batman and Rambo movies and comics. Confronting anyone armed with assault weapons is asking for an early grave. The most sensible thing to do is get out of the way.

Civilians Preventing Massacres

Not a single mass shooting since 1982 has been prevented by an armed civilian, despite the 310m guns owned in America.

In two school shootings in the 1990's, in Pennsylvania and Mississippi, armed civilians apprehended the assailant only after the shooting was over. In neither case did the civilians intervene to prevent the massacre[14].

In 2005 during a mall rampage in Tacoma, Washington, a civilian, Brendan McKown, confronted the killer with a licensed handgun. The assailant shot McKown multiple times and wounded six bystanders before being apprehended by authorities.

In Tyler, Texas, Mark Wilson, a civilian, fired at an assailant in the county courthouse who was wearing body armor and carrying an AK-47. The assailant shot and killed Wilson, a firearm instructor.

In 2002 at the Appalachian School of Law in Virginia, armed students apprehended the killer during a massacre. This case is often used as evidence that arming students would lead to fewer incidents and fewer people killed. It turned out that the killer was out of ammunition by the time he was apprehended, and the students were actually current and former law enforcement officers, not civilians.

Law enforcement prefers that civilian's retreat from mass shootings rather than attempt to get involved. At no point do most law enforcement agencies advise civilians to intervene in mass shootings. Most law enforcement officers recognize the danger of weapons especially assault rifles, being in the hands of assailants.

Massacres and Mental Illness

There is some evidence to suggest that some of these mass killers may have had mental illness ranging from paranoid schizophrenia to suicidal depression. Many of the mass killers in the past thirty years have shown signs of mental instability. However, there is little evidence to suggest that their mental illness, if any, was responsible for the mass shooting, or that people with mental illness present a greater threat to society than citizens without these issues.

While many point to the fact that many of the killers displayed mental health issues, this is not necessarily the common thread binding all these killers together. The single distinguishing feature of all these killers was possession of and access to firearms. If firearms had not been available to these killers, 524 people could well be alive today. Many of these killers carefully planned the event, but some single event appeared to spark the massacre. The most common predictor was the loss of a job, in about 47 cases, while divorce or break up was common in 22 cases[15].

Mental illness did appear to play some role, with at least half of all mass killers having histories of mental health problems, including hospitalization, prescriptions for psychiatric drugs, suicide attempts or some evidence of psychosis. Some studies indicate that the mentally ill are no more violent than others are unless they are off their medications, or abusing drugs or alcohol.

Press Coverage as a Cause

There is some debate as to whether publicity surrounding mass shootings may cause other mass shootings[16]. If that were true, there ought to be a spate of mass shootings in rapid succession, which generally does not appear to happen, since these incidents are often separated by a number of months or years. The apparent links between events appears tenuous at best. Due to their proximity, some speculate that given the short time between the massacre in Dunblane, Scotland and the killing in Port Arthur, Tasmania, the Port Arthur killer was influenced by the Dunblane killer. This is a tenuous connection at best, with little evidence to suggest that one massacre caused the other.

The claim that this raises an ethical dilemma for the media seems ill placed. The media are no more responsible for gun massacres than they are for car accidents, wars, assaults or other crimes on which they also report. There may be some residual effect in some cases, but it is far more likely that the perpetrators have other reasons for their actions. Any attempt to blame media is just a way to divert attention from the proximate cause, which is access to weapons. Without those weapons, even if perpetrators of mass murder were copying others, it would still be far more difficult for them to kill a great number of people.

Politicizing the Tragedy

When gun massacres like Aurora and Newtown happen, the first response of the gun lobby is likely to be, do not politicize the tragedy. In essence, they are saying, do not talk about controlling our guns. It is rather like saying after a hurricane; lets not talk about the loss of life and property in Congress out of respect for the survivors.

The right time to tackle important laws like gun regulation is when there is a tragedy, when it is still fresh in peoples minds, and before they go on to more trivial pursuits. The gun lobby is successfully politicizing the event with their words, just because they do not want the problem handled in a rational, sensible fashion. We can talk about other issues such as infrastructure collapse when they happen, but not gun violence. This is another clear demonstration of the morally inconsistent stance taken by the gun lobby, members of Congress, and the rest of the gun industry.

Massacres are Increasing

What is disturbing about massacres is that they appear to be increasing in number, albeit from an extremely low level, about one tenth of one percent of all homicides. In the last few years, those numbers have risen. This reflects the nationwide trend towards more lethal weapons and higher capacity magazines. The production of semi automatic weapons now exceeds the production of revolvers. Semi-automatics have a greater magazine capacity, and are faster to reload, enabling mass killers to kill a greater number of people.

One study of active shooter events between 2000 and 2010 concluded that public rampage shootings have spiked over the last few years; many of the attackers were heavily armed and no civilian with a firearm prevented even one[17]. None of the studies of mass shootings includes criminal related shootings, such as those perpetrated by gangs. In 41% of attacks, the shooters carried multiple weapons and 60% carried pistols. There are still insufficient data to state categorically that massacres are increasing, given that they are low probability events. That is not to imply that they are rare events; in comparison to other industrialized countries, mass shootings are all too common.

Dismissing Massacres as Aberrations

What is equally disturbing is that many commentators, often on the right, dismiss mass shootings as aberrations because there are so few of them. These pundits, often self-appointed, refuse to make substantive changes to gun laws in spite of the relative horror of mass shootings by claiming that mass shootings are irrelevant relative to other forms of death[18]. These arguments take various forms, but reduce to the same idea, that since death by drowning, vehicles, or knives is greater than by firearm, we can easily forget the horror perpetrated by people with assault weapons or high capacity magazines. Many forget that mass shootings are just part of a larger mosaic of gun homicide, suicide and ubiquitous gun violence.

The very idea that we can reduce death by banning or severely limiting these destructive weapons is anathema to critics of gun regulation when compared to the sanctity of the Second Amendment. It does not strike them that we should be doing whatever we can to reduce unnecessary death by any method. Death by firearm is not purely unnecessary; it is also easily preventable by banning firearms. It is morally abhorrent that we should ignore certain deaths because there are so few; we demand safety standards for aircraft, despite there being so few deaths, and for strangulation by perambulators, despite there being only one or two such deaths each year, and we do it because it is the morally correct thing to do. Perambulators and aircraft are necessary to our modern lives whereas firearms have no place in a peaceful, civilized society.

The Rush to Arm After Massacres

In the wake of a massacre there is inevitably a rush to buy even more firearms, pouring even more fuel on the conflagration of gun violence. The gun industry relishes these massacres because it pads their revenues. All they need do is wait it out while the bluster and braggadocio dies down, secure in the knowledge that gullible citizens, scared to death will flow in to spend dollars on worthless firearms, paradoxically increasing their risk of violent death.

Critics of gun restrictions claim that various suggested controls would not prevent gun massacres. These controls include enhanced background checks, better mental health screenings, banning assault weapons, increasing school security, or security drills in schools. Like any relatively complex problem in society, we need to have a multi-faceted approach to prevention and regulation, and accept that not all massacres or gun violence will be prevented. What we seek, as with any social disease, is a reduction in gun violence and crime, not a panacea. Having said that, societies like Japan and the United Kingdom have managed to reduce gun violence to the point that it is almost non-existent.

Silence From Anti-Gun-Violence Advocates

The relative silence from gun regulation advocates, despite the enormous numbers of people murdered each year with firearms, or those who take their own lives, or the accidental deaths and injuries due to these weapons, is deafening. The pro-gun lobby has so intimidated anti-gun-violence advocates especially those in public office and so dominated the public debate, that few are willing to speak out publicly against the gun industry for fear of losing their seats in Congress.

The gun lobby, headed by the NRA and its powerful associated organization, ALEC, has vastly greater financial muscle than does the gun regulation lobby. Legislators have been openly threatened with the loss of their seats by this arm of the gun industry. The anti-gun-violence lobby simply cannot compete with the financial resources of the gun industry, which has managed to shift public opinion in favor of relaxed gun laws.

Despite increasing numbers of gun massacres, Democrats, traditionally opposed to neglectful gun laws, are doing nothing to prevent the violence against innocent civilians. President Obama and other Democrats have had nothing to say about gun regulation, despite the death toll, for fear of the gun industry. The NRA raised $253 million from supporters in 2010, while the Brady Center to Prevent Gun Violence raised about $6 million. After the shooting of Rep. Gabrielle Giffords in Tucson, Arizona, which should have heightened awareness of gun violence, almost nothing was done to change the gun dynamic.

The Massacres

Newtown, Connecticut

The Newtown massacre had a profound impact on my life. The images of twenty children and the teachers that perished protecting them are forever seared on my brain. That Congress was incapable of taking meaningful action to prevent massacres and other gun violence despite the slaughter of children, still angers me.

Adam Lanza, the twenty-year-old killer of twenty elementary school children and six teaching staff at the Sandy Hook Elementary School in Newtown Connecticut, was a young man obsessed with weapons. Warrant affidavits unsealed by a judge in Danbury on March 28th 2013, paint a chilling portrait of a man whose obsession would end the lives of these young children and their teachers.

Investigators found an empty box for Battle Tested vest accessories and hundreds of rounds of ammunition of various types in his home[1]. Lanza had receipts and emails documenting his firearm and ammunition purchases. Paperwork from the Connecticut Gun Exchange documented the Glock 20SF he used in the shootings. Investigators seized an NRA guide on the basics of pistol shooting and an NRA certificate for Nancy Lanza, his mother, from his home. He kept a receipt for the Timstar Shooting Range. Investigators found three photographs of a deceased human covered in plastic and what appears to be blood. His mother, Nancy, gave him a holiday card with a check for the purchase of a C183 firearm.

Also recovered by police were a Samurai sword, a long pole with a blade on one side and spear on the other and a variety of blade weapons. In the killers' car were a 12-gauge shotgun and two magazines containing 70 rounds of ammunition. Lanza was dressed in military style clothing wearing a bulletproof vest during the massacre. He had with him an assault style weapon and several handguns. In all, Lanza had access to over 1700 rounds of ammunition.

Lanza researched mass shootings for years[2]. Police discovered a spreadsheet seven feet long and four feet wide containing details about the names and number of people killed, the weapons used and the make and model of the weapons. Law enforcement officials claimed that it resembled a doctoral thesis. Given this evidence, and the planning that he put into his attack, it is exceedingly unlikely that Lanza was suffering from any readily identifiable mental illness that led to the massacre. Lanza showed every indication of a detailed, organized mind, the ability to maintain focus and to plan long-term, not the disjointed, disordered thinking of a person with severe mental illness.

First responders in Newtown have quit their jobs because of what they saw that morning. Teachers were found with their arms wrapped around the children they tried to save. Some law enforcement officials believe that Lanza saw his massacre as a video game, in which his intent was to get to the top of the massacre score sheet. These officials speculate that he saw the elementary school as the easiest target to rack up his kills. This line of speculation posits that he killed himself because he did not want law enforcement to take his life, given that in some video games if your character dies, you forfeit your points to your opponent. This speculation in no way explains, justifies, or prevents situations like this from developing in the future.

It is unlikely that Lanza experienced a psychotic break; he had carefully planned the massacre for years. He was easily able to get hold of these deadly weapons, one of them an AR-15, from his survivalist mother. He allegedly learned some of his techniques from video games, in which, like police, he would eject his magazine after shooting in one room, even though it had 15 rounds left in it and reload before entering the next room, leaving him with a full magazine. This is known as the tactical reload. When the strap broke on his AR-15, he went to his handgun, which is classic police training.

Lanza's mother had been making straw purchases for her son, and actively encouraging his gun obsession. Law enforcement said that the school did everything they could, and they saved many lives acting the way they did; little else other than comprehensive gun regulation might have salvaged the situation.

The reaction to the shooting was predictable. The President came out and said[3],

> "We are going to have to come together and take meaningful action to prevent more tragedies like this, regardless of the politics."

The President also expressed *"enormous sympathy for the families that are affected"*. Flags flew at half-staff at the White House and other federal buildings. The President flew to Connecticut and spoke at a vigil for the victims, honoring the six school staff killed with the Presidential Citizens Medal. The governor of Connecticut urged the people to come together and help each other[4],

> "Evil visited this community today and it is too early to speak of recovery, but each parent, each sibling, each member of the family has to understand that Connecticut, we are all in this together, we will do whatever we can to overcome this event, we will get through it."

The governor called for a moment of silence and church bells rang 26 times. The U.S. secretary of Education said,

> "Our thanks go out to every teacher, staff member, and first responded who cared for, comforted and protected children from harm often at risk to themselves. We

will do everything in our power to assist and support the healing and recover of Newtown."

Lanza's father released a statement,

"Our hearts go out to the families and friends who lost loved ones and to all those who were injured. Our family is grieving along with all those who have been affected by this enormous tragedy...."

The President called for using *"whatever power this office holds to prevent similar tragedies in the future"*, pledging to make gun regulation a *"central issue"* during his second term. The president issued 23 executive orders. Dianne Feinstein proposed an assault weapons ban. The Manchin-Toomey Background checks Bill failed to pass the U.S. Senate on April 17.

Jay Carney, Obama's spokesman said,

"This is not a day for a debate on gun control."

If not today, then perhaps we should wait a month, two, or when everyone has forgotten the incident. This is what the gun industry and the gun lobby count on, the capricious state of people's memories and emotions.

The noted conspiracy theorist, Alex Jones, claimed that the Newtown massacre was staged, without producing any evidence.

The reaction to the shooting was mostly predictable, worthless and short. A year after the tragedy, not a single line of legislation has passed the U.S. Senate, with no whisper of action in the House. It helps not one whit to make bold pronouncements about coming together, or praying and grieving for the victims. Claims that the people are in it together are empty gestures, and do nothing whatsoever to honor the victims. Moments of silence are utterly prosaic and meaningless in the face of continuing gun violence. The only single measure that would help is comprehensive gun limitation legislation, as happened in Connecticut where restrictions on weapons and LCM's passed the state legislature.

All the tears, the condemnations, the shock, heartbreak, appeals to evil and moral posturing are worthless. It is only when the American people tire of the ceaseless violence and death by firearm, when those deaths become more important than clinging to extreme weapons that perhaps we will see change.

What was striking in the aftermath of this tragedy was the complete absence of empathy from the gun industry, the gun lobby, and especially Republican members of Congress. In Colorado, unsympathetic voters recalled two state senators because of their vote in favor of sane, stricter gun laws while another lawmaker resigned rather than face a recall vote. Despite the continuing tragedy of gun deaths, conservatives and gun proponents demand continuing access to extreme firearms. Every gun massacre brings the same trite, hackneyed platitudes, the same rush to buy more guns, and no action other than more lenient laws in states entirely lacking in moral fortitude, almost invariably the South, Midwest and Mountain-West.

The true heroes of this massacre were the teachers - public servants who are incessantly targeted, denigrated and blamed for all society's ills. When budgets are cut, teachers are often the first to go despite the essential role they play in educating society. Conservatives routinely attack teachers to establish their bona fides. During this massacre, they threw themselves onto their children, or hugged them close or tried to block the gunman, to save their children. These are the true brave souls, far more so than those who only demand more firearms in schools.

Las Vegas Shooting

On September 25th, 2017, Stephen Paddock entered the Mandalay Bay Hotel in Las Vegas Nevada. Over the course of four days, he stockpiled 10 AR-15 rifles with 100-round magazines in his room and the room adjoining his.

He chose this venue over other venues that he had researched in cities like Boston. In Las Vegas, he examined a number of hotels overlooking open-air venues, including the *"Life is Beautiful"* festival.

On October 1st, at 10:05 p.m., Paddock used a hammer to break two windows in each of his suites. He began by firing single gunshots before firing with longer bursts. He used a bump-fire stock, which increases the rate at which a semi-automatic weapon can be fired, essentially creating an automatic weapon.

People at the Route 91 Harvest country music festival believed at first that the gunshots were fireworks. By the time the shooting ended at 10:05 p.m., 31 people were dead, and 27 later died of their injuries.

When police officers arrived, they could not immediately determine whether the shots were coming from the Mandalay Bay Hotel, The Luxor, or the festival grounds. Multiple false claims of shooters at other hotels on the strip also came in to officers. It was only when two officers on the 31st floor of the Mandalay Bay Hotel reported shots fired from the floor above them that police could pinpoint the shooter.

A hotel security guard injured by Paddock directed officers to his room. At 10:26 p.m., eight additional officers arrived on the 32nd floor and breached the door to Paddock's room. The shooter was found dead from a self-inflicted gunshot wound to the head.

A total of 851 people were injured, 422 with gunshot wounds, in addition to the fatalities.

Las Vegas Boulevard was closed as police searched businesses. All four runways at McCarran International Airport were closed for fear of gunfire. At 2:45 p.m., a state of emergency was declared in Clark County, fourteen hours after the shooting.

The reactions from various quarters were disappointingly predictable. Trolls on 4chan, a political imageboard, immediately claimed that the shooter was a registered Democrat[5]. A conservative reporter published an article making the same claim, and then later retracted it. Facebook and Twitter accounts claimed that the shooter was part of the leftist group Antifa[6].

A fake news website claimed falsely that a second gunman was shooting from the fourth floor of the hotel. Google promoted the news to the top of its search results before it was debunked[7].

Trending pages on Facebook were linked to Sputnik, a Russian government news agency. One of these pages claimed that the FBI had linked the shooter to a terrorist group[8].

Alex Jones, a conservative conspiracy theorist immediately tied the shooter to the terror group, ISIS, and also to a communist takeover over the United States. Even Scott Adams, creator of the comic strip Dilbert, claimed that the shooter was *"probably associated with the left, maybe it's Antifa, maybe it's ISIS, maybe just anti-Trump"*.

It strikes me as somewhat ironic that conservative outlets would try to pin the blame for this heinous act on liberals. Many conservatives decry the politicizing of massacres and yet some blame the tragedies on their political opponents without evidence.

Despite ISIS claiming that Paddock was a member, no evidence was ever produced to verify their claim. The terror group has tried this for other incidents with which they have no connection. The FBI found no evi0dence of any ties to the group, but some right-leaning outlets claimed that the shooter had converted to Islam before the attacks[9].

Chris Murphy, the Senator from Connecticut said, *"It is time for Congress to get off its ass and do something"*. Secretary Hillary Clinton said, *"Our grief is not enough"*.

The reaction from Michelle Obama epitomized the reaction on the left. She said that much of the role of commander in chief is,

"Overseeing that kind of loss and really not having a solution to offer families when you comfort them"

A Trump White House memo opposed tightening gun laws because,

"New laws won't stop a madman committed to harming innocent people. They will curtail the freedoms of law abiding citizens".

This type of reaction shows that many conservatives have little interest in finding solutions to massacres.

Donald Trump himself was asked about changes in the law and he responded[10],

"We're not going to talk about that today. We won't talk about that"

A month later, an Uzbek man killed 8 people in New York City with a truck. Trump responded that,

"The man came into our country through what is called the 'Diversity Visa Lottery Program' a Chuck Schumer Beauty. I want merit based"

Trump had almost nothing to say about the 58 victims in Las Vegas, but in essence blamed an attack by one man on the immigrant community, and Democrats. This kind of unwarranted ideological attack does little to mitigate the threat to peace from gun violence.

Congress was unable to enact laws prohibiting the sale of bump fire stocks, despite two bipartisan bills introduced in the House. Instead, House leaders passed the ball to the Bureau of Alcohol, Tobacco and Firearms. Paul Ryan claimed that,

"This is a regulation that probably shouldn't have happened in the first place"

Instead of taking action, GOP leaders blamed the Obama administration for the sale of the device. Yet, Congress still failed to pass legislation. It is within their power to do so. Blaming the opposition may be an effective tactic, but it is not ethical[11].

The death of 58 people, and the injuring of 851, still has not spurred Congress into any kind of action. The Congress and the executive, along with the Courts are entrusted with the power to enact meaningful restrictions. Despite this, they have only succeeded in abrogating more power to the gun lobby.

Democratic senators introduced a bill, the Keep Americans Safe Act, which would ban magazines holding more than ten rounds. The bill, predictably, went nowhere[12].

Stock prices of gun manufacturers rose in anticipation of a wave of firearm purchases. This typically happens in the wake of a massacre, because many people believe that firearms will be restricted.

Survivors of the shooting received death threats on social media. In addition, they were accused of being paid actors[13]. One victim who escaped death had to shut down his social media accounts. The bullying has spread to family and friends.

Yet again, Congress dismissed the massacre, the media forgot it and moved on, and the Left got the blame. The victims will receive no justice, but are left with the scars, the bills, and the memories.

Orlando Nightclub Shooting

On June 12th, 2016, Omar Mateen entered the Pulse nightclub in Orlando, Florida, armed with a SIG Sauer semi-automatic rifle, and took the lives of 49 people, injuring 58 others. It took the Orlando Police Department three hours to end his killing spree. By far the greatest number of victims were Hispanic, since the club was hosting a "Latin Night"

Mateen declared his allegiance to the Islamic State in a call to 911[14]. In a call to a hostage negotiator, he claimed that the killing spree was due to American invasions of Iraq and Syria.

In the aftermath of the massacre, claims were made that Mateen was a frequent visitor to the nightclub, but no credible evidence was found to substantiate the claim.

One security guard and two police officers initially engaged the shooter, who retreated further into the building. Over 45 minutes, more than 100 officers were dispatched to the scene in addition to at least eighty Fire and Emergency personnel from the Orlando fire department

Inside the building, panicked revelers issued a torrent of text messages to friends and families. As with other tragedies of the sort, many initially thought that the gunshots were firecrackers and did not respond.

A marine veteran who recognized the sounds leaped over a locked door to allow dozens of people paralyzed with fear to escape the massacre. Inside, people hid beneath bodies to escape detection.

Inside a bathroom, fifteen people hid as the gunman fired through the door, killing two people.

The loud music and darkness served to confuse people and create even more panic and chaos.

President Obama, in his reaction to the shooting, said[15],

> "This massacre is therefore a further reminder of how easy it is for someone to get their hands on a weapon that lets them shoot people in a school or in a house of worship or a movie theater or a nightclub. And we have to decide if that's the kind of country we want to be. And to actively do nothing is a decision as well."

Consider the implications of this massacre. Mateen encountered an armed security guard on entering the club. Despite being an off-duty police officer who exchanged gunfire with the shooter, the guard was unable to stop the massacre[16]. Six officers, including some armed with assault rifles, shot out a window and followed the sound of gunfire into the building. They had difficulty locating the shooter – people were screaming and shots were heard. Two of the officers shot at the assailant. The officers were ordered to hold position instead of storming the building[17].

Around twenty minutes later, a SWAT team arrived and had the officers withdraw because they were not dressed in tactical gear.

Despite being armed and trained, the first few officers were unable to stop the shooter. Even with a full tactical SWAT team, the shooter was still able to continue his rampage. The entire event lasted at least three hours before police stormed the building and killed the assailant.

The latest pearls of wisdom from Donald Trump include arming teachers to prevent attacks like these. If law enforcement officers armed with assault rifles were unable to storm the building and stop the shooter, what chance would a group of schoolteachers have in a similar position? Trained officers could not summon the courage to engage with the shooter, and yet people expect teachers to put their own lives in danger to engage a man armed with an assault rifle.

It takes a lot of courage to face down someone armed with a military-style weapon. To expect a teacher to do this armed with no more than a handgun is patently absurd. Consider the environment, panicked victims, darkness, a lack of intelligence as to the shooters whereabouts. A shooter armed with an assault weapon. There is no reasonable way for ordinary civilians to expect to prevent a shooting of this type.

Attacks of this type are a clear indication of how difficult it is to prevent a determined attacker armed with assault weapons from harming civilians. Most spree killers expect to lose their lives, and will not be deterred by a few people armed with concealed weapons. At least one hundred officers dispatched to the scene were unable to prevent more deaths.

The three-hour standoff prevented emergency personnel from entering the building to treat the wounded. At least five people still alive when the standoff started ultimately died because of the inaction of law enforcement[18]. The inexplicable delay probably caused more loss of life. This was despite the enormous number of officers at the scene.

The Orlando Police Department is upgrading its equipment, because officers were insufficiently equipped. This increases the burden on taxpayers, instead of tackling the root cause of the massacre.

Two of the hospitals that treated the victims will not be billing victims for their injuries[19]. This is another cost that others have to pay. Additional costs were incurred through groups raising money for the victims. Buddy Dyer, the Orlando Mayor, established OneOrlando, a fundraising campaign. The charity managed to raise at least $23 million. These costs are borne by the community instead of by gun owners.

The City of Orlando paid $4,518 to place a fence, with a commemorative wrap to serve as a memorial to the victims[20]. The City also announced plans to purchase the club and create a permanent memorial. The owner declined to sell.

Governor Scott ordered 49 flags flown for 49 days in front of the Capitol in Tallahassee, along with photos of the wounded. The Mayor of Orlando, Buddy Dyer declared a state of emergency. President Obama ordered the *"federal government to provide any assistance necessary to pursue the investigation and support the community"*

This incident shows just how difficult it is to take action to prevent a massacre. The idea that revelers armed with handguns would have prevented this attack is just ludicrous. In the confusion of a darkened nightclub, with flashing lights, smoke, loud music and gunfire, it is highly unlikely that armed attendees would have prevented deaths. The presence of arms in a highly charged environment is only likely to exacerbate the destruction. There is no reasonable way that armed men could know who the killer was. Introducing more firearms makes it increasingly less likely that the shooter will be recognized. It is far better to prevent massacres before they happen, by taking concerted action against firearm ownership.

The shooting was the deadliest in American history at the time. A mere fifteen months later, that record was smashed in Las Vegas.

Stoneman Douglas High School

On February 14th, 2018, Nikolas Jacob Cruz took the lives of seventeen people, and injured sixteen more in the Stoneman Douglas High School. This makes it one of the world's most deadly school massacres. Six of the top 15 deadliest school massacres on Earth have happened in the United States[21]. Every single one of those fifteen massacres involved the use of at least one firearm.

The shooter entered the school building and activated a fire alarm[22]. This caused confusion among students because there was a fire drill earlier in the day. People leaving the building increased the confusion. When students returned to the building, the gunman followed them in. After the shooting, the killer dropped his weapon, and blended in with students streaming away from the school.

Two teachers were killed protecting their students. Another lost his life running towards the sound of gunfire to help students. A fifteen-year-old student died holding open doors to allow others to escape[23]. A petition is circulating to award the student posthumous military honors.

A school resource officer at the scene did not enter the building to engage the shooter. He claimed that he thought the shots were coming from outside the building[24]. This shows again why it is so difficult to react during a crisis like this. It is not clear where shots are coming from, and every human's instinctive first reaction is self-preservation. The officer, despite being trained was unable to prevent the deaths.

An assessment of the killer, who previously received mental health treatment, found that he was *"at low risk of harming himself or others"*. That assessment was incorrect, which shows just how difficult it is to use mental health screening to deter potential killers. Even considering their right to due process, condemning large numbers of people based on an assessment is not practical. The logistics of testing tens of millions of people are not feasible. This is just a distraction in the ongoing battle against gun violence.

President Trump claimed, implausibly, that he would have charged in, even unarmed. The president clearly does not comprehend just how difficult it is for anyone to face down a well-armed spree shooter.

People who present solutions like arming teachers or hiring security guards do not comprehend the difficulty of situations like this. Spree killers are often not afraid to lose their lives; often that is their desire. Armed teachers or guards are not going to deter them from their objective. Chaotic scenes are difficult for anyone to understand. This is known as the "fog of war". Even seasoned veterans have great difficulty discerning where a threat originates and countering that threat.

Honoring the heroes of massacres like this is laudable. What is far more important is to reduce access to firearms throughout the United States. That is the most effective way to honor the victims of America's ceaseless gun violence. Only by reducing the availability of firearms can we hope to reduce the deaths and injuries. That is the most sensible way to honor the dead.

Virginia Tech, Virginia

In 2007, Seung-Hui Cho took 33 lives on the Virginia Tech Campus, the deadliest shooting in the United States for many years. After the tragic shooting spree, lawmakers did nothing to change the gun laws in their state. The rampant private trade in guns continues. Last year, legislation passed allowing people with concealed weapons permits to carry their weapons into bars and restaurants, provided they are not drinking alcohol. Open carry laws now allow people to carry their weapons into state parks[25].

The Virginia State governor declared a state of emergency allowing him to deploy state personnel, equipment and other resources[26]. The gunman had taken his own life, so was no longer a threat. It is difficult to see of what value these measures were. Far better would have been to empanel a committee tasked with reducing gun violence through strict gun regulation.

The gun lobby actually pushed legislation to allow guns on college campuses. After the tragedy that happened in Virginia Tech, you would think that everything would be done to get guns off campus, Instead, the gun lobby wants increased access to guns in schools, colleges and universities. Their insensibility to tragedy and suffering is difficult to comprehend. Firearms have no place in schools or on college campuses, and attempts to force institutes of learning to allow students to carry will only end in more death and bloodshed. A large number of armed students attempting to intervene during a mass shooting would inevitably end in a greater massacre, as is invariably the case during chaotic events.

The only thing to come of the death of so many at the school was a minor tightening up of background checks for the mentally ill under the NICS background check system and a halt in sales to criminals. Other than that, it is as though the tragedy never happened. The condolences offered by other colleges may have made them feel better, but ultimately they did nothing to resolve the underlying problem of gun violence. The university did introduce an alert system on their website and text messaging to warn students of danger[27].

Luby's Massacre

In 1991, George Pierre Hennard crashed his Ford Ranger pickup through the front window of a Luby's cafeteria in Killeen, Texas. He proceeded to slaughter 23 people and injure a further 27. After engaging in a firefight with police, he barricaded himself inside a bathroom and took his own life. He reloaded his weapons several times and still had ammunition when he took his life.

Texas, in response, did nothing to mitigate gun violence or prevent people like Hennard from possessing firearms. Instead, they introduced a Shall-Issue law, requiring that all qualified applicants be issued a concealed carry permit, making it easier for future Hennard to carry firearms into restaurants. The criteria included being free of felony conviction, taking a 10-hour course, passing a 50-question test, showing proficiency in a 50 round shooting test and passing two background checks. Shall-Issue laws remove the discretion of the issuing authority to deny licenses. A survivor who did not have a firearm with her, instead leaving it in her vehicle, pushed for passage of the law.

Hennard, like many mass killers, was intensely hostile towards women. Survivors said that Hennard allowed some men to live in order to murder the women in the restaurant. Instead of introducing a law allowing more firearms on the street, a law testing firearm owners for signs of paranoia, hatred and anger might have saved more lives. Far too many gun owners harbor hatred towards groups including women, foreigners, immigrants or those who speak or look different.

McDonalds in San Ysidro[28]

In July 1984, James Oliver Huberty entered a McDonalds in San Ysidro and murdered 21 people, including five children, grandmothers, infants and employees. The killer had a history of violence against his wife, also a violent woman who once threatened the mother of a neighbor with a 9mm pistol. Huberty once killed his own dog after complaints by a neighbor. When he was younger, the killer's mother had abandoned him to spend her time preaching on the sidewalk for the Southern Baptists.

Like Nancy Lanza, the Newtown killers' mother, Huberty was a survivalist who believed that government was the cause of his travails, including a failed business venture. He believed that international bankers were manipulating the Federal Reserve and bankrupting the nation, a fatuous belief common among conservatives, survivalists and militia groups. He also believed that Soviet aggression was everywhere, and that societal breakdown would occur through nuclear war or economic breakdown.

Like many survivalists, he provisioned his home with non-perishables for the coming chaos. Before his killing spree, he told his wife he was "hunting humans", and that society had "had its chance".

As with many other mass killers, his weapon of choice was a semi-automatic, in this case a 9mm long barrel Uzi, as well as a Winchester 12 gauge pump-action shotgun and a 9mm Browning pistol. During his rampage, he expended 257 rounds of ammunition before a SWAT sniper finally fatally shot him from a nearby Post Office.

The first armed individual on the scene was a police officer who believed that he was responding to a single gunshot incident. His standard .38 revolver left him totally outgunned by the killer. Hubert was firing armor-piercing rounds at the officer, who had no defense, despite protestations of good guys with guns stopping bad guys with guns.

The reaction followed the standard banal progression. San Diego police increased special unit training, along with more powerful firearms to cater for future incidents. Across the country, similar reactions occurred in police departments. Departments requested armed officers with higher power firearms, and training for stopping violent criminals, as well as dedicated full-time, well-trained and well-equipped teams.

In order to prevent violence from people who have free access to extreme firearms, society must arm, train and equip more people with extreme weapons, wasting more resources because of the manic insistence on firearms by the gun lobby. Police departments are forced to learn about these incidents in real time, given the complete lack of research departments, paying with lives and blood.

McDonalds, naturally, was cleared of any responsibility for the incident since they have no duty to protect patrons. The plaintiffs could not prove causation because of the presence of video surveillance. In the case of school shootings, the NRA demanded armed guards; it is surprising that they did not demand the same of fast food restaurants.

Sutherland Springs Church Shooting

On November 5th, 2017, Devin Patrick Kelley killed 26 people and injured 20 others. In the First Baptist Church in Sutherland Springs, Texas. The massacre was the deadliest shooting in any place of worship in the United States.

The perpetrator was denied the right to purchase a firearm because he was convicted on domestic violence while serving in the United States Air Force. However, the Air Force failed to record his conviction in the FBI database. This data is used to deny the purchase of firearms. It was due to their dereliction of duty that the perpetrator was able to take so many lives.

During the attack, Kelley wore black tactical gear, a ballistic vest and black facemask with the image of a white skull. Inside, worshipers were at a regular Sunday service. He entered the church and systematically shot people in the pews.

As the killer left the church, he traded gunfire with a local resident. The resident, a firearm instructor was armed with an AR-15 and shot the killer once in the leg and upper torso.

The killer fled the scene in a Ford Explorer, pursued by the instructor. The killer was later found dead in his Explorer. The killing spree was sparked by a dispute with the killers' mother-in-law.

Kelley had a history of violent behavior. He was charged with assaulting his wife and fracturing his stepson's skull. His superior officers charged him with assault. Kelley then threatened his superiors and smuggled firearms onto the base.

His wife lived in fear of her husband. At one point, he threatened to kill her entire family and she finally divorced him.

His life did not improve on dismissal from the Air Force. He was investigated for rape, sexual assault and assault on his girlfriend. In court filings, his ex-wife claimed that, *"for a whole year, he slapped me, choked me, kicked me, water-boarded me and held a gun to my head."*

He purchased his firearm by lying about his previous criminal conviction. Texas denied his application for a license to carry a firearm, but the state does not require a license to purchase firearms. Nonetheless, he should have failed the background check because of his conviction.

President Trump issued this statement,

> "I think that mental health is a problem here. Based on preliminary reports, this was a very deranged individual with a lot of problems over a very long period of time. We have a lot of mental health problems in our country, as do other countries, but this isn't a guns situation ... we could go into it but it's a little bit soon to go into it. Fortunately somebody else had a gun that was shooting in the

opposite direction, otherwise it wouldn't have been as bad as it was, it would have been much worse"

The President claimed that extreme vetting would have made *"no difference"*, He also claim that stricter gun control would have prevented the firearm instructor from engaging the killer. *"Instead of 26 dead, we would have had hundreds"*

The Texas Attorney General proposed that all churches employ armed security guards, or arm more parishioners. He claimed that church shootings have happened forever and will again. The Democratic Party executive director said, *"Texans deserve more from their chief law enforcement official than inaction and willful ignorance"*

The pastor claimed that the church would be demolished to make way for a prayer garden, saying that it would be too painful to continue using it as a place of worship[29]. Later that same month, the pastor claimed that the news reports were false and that a decision had not yet been made[30].

The reaction to the shooting followed a similar pattern to other shootings. In the hours following an attack, conspiracy theories fly think and fast. A Congressman from Texas blamed a man named Sam Hyde for the massacre[31]. Sam Hyde is an Internet hoax that appears during mass shootings; he has been blamed for the shooting in Las Vegas, San Bernadino, Minneapolis and Kalamazoo. Sam Hyde does not exist other than on right-wing web sites like 4chan.

Other people claim that the shooting was a conspiracy to manipulate the public. This was even heard from families of the victims.

On the far right, a number of groups were blamed, including Antifa and Muslims. This despite a lack of evidence that he was affiliated with either[32]. Some even claimed that he forced his victims to read from communist texts and targeted the church because it was a "white conservative" organization. It is a shame that a tragedy like this is used to promote a conservative agenda.

Law enforcement still does not know what the killer's motives were. He was not affiliated with any leftist or terrorist groups that we know of. He had no connection to Democrats or Hillary Clinton.

The President's statements did not agree with the facts. This is most definitely a guns situation. The lax laws in the United States allowed this man to get a firearm and take the lives of 26 people. Without that access, he would have found it very difficult to do.

The mental health system did nothing to ensure that society would be safe from this man. There is no way to know who will become violent other than through a pattern of behavior, as the killer clearly demonstrated. If domestic abuse were a criterion for denying access to firearms, he may have been prevented from obtaining firearms.

The President's statement about someone shooting in the opposite direction is similarly misleading. The shooter had already finished his rampage. The firearm instructor did not prevent the tragedy; he merely killed the shooter after the fact.

The idea that armed security guards be placed at the church is similarly impractical. According to the National Congregations Study (NCS), there were 384,000 congregations in the U.S. in 2012[33]. Using a similar methodology to that used for schools, how much would it cost to employ security guards at all churches?

Given an hourly rate of $25, for 52 days, and at least 6 hours per day, each church would pay $7,800 per year for a single guard. If two guards are used, that figure is $15,600. For a single guard for all congregations, the cost is $3 billion dollars per year; for two guards, $6Bn. The cost rises with the size of the building.

Many churches have separate facilities for Sunday school or other activities. That means that each building must have multiple guards. This does not include the cost of firearms, ammunition, and training.

Additionally, a traditional security guard just does not have the training to engage a well-armed spree killer. There is no reason that a security guard should put his life in danger for the normal wage of $12 per hour. That means hiring law enforcement, which is more expensive.

With each massacre, the idea of introducing security guards comes up. With each massacre, the potential costs spiral upwards. Schools, churches, nightclubs, workplaces, or any other area where people gather are also vulnerable. That includes sports stadiums, amusement parks, shopping malls, universities, train and bus stations, and concerts. The potential costs of providing security guards at all these venues will eventually become an enormous drain on the economy. Until we tackle the 800-pound gorilla in the room, people will continue to lose their lives.

We do not want a security state in which armed guards are everywhere. This does not make society safer; it only increases the risks of people being shot, and of increasingly oppressive and militarized societies.

San Bernadino

On the 2nd October, 2015, 14 people lost their lives, and 22 were seriously injured. A married couple, Syed Rizwan Farook and Tashfeen Malik, entered a Department of Public Health training event and Christmas party banquet hall and massacred revelers.

The couple claimed to be part of a foreign terror group. Law enforcement determined that they were homegrown extremists. A search of their home found a stockpile of weapons, ammunition and bomb-making equipment. The attack was the most deadly terrorist attack since 9/11.

The two assailants wore ski masks and black tactical gear that included load-bearing vests containing magazines and ammunition. The assault took only two or three minutes during which 14 people lost their lives. People were hiding under tables, or in closets, bathrooms and cupboards. The shooters moved around the room shooting anyone who made a sound.

One bullet penetrated an interior wall, striking one victim. Another tried to escape through a glass door and was shot. Three men attempted to stop the shooters; all were shot. It is unclear whether they survived. One person died trying to shield another with his body.

The first police unit took more than three minutes to respond to the shooting, by which time the attack was effectively over. When first responders entered the building, they ignored the pleas of victims for assistance and continued to search for the shooters, who had already left the building.

After a chaotic search, the two killers were killed by law enforcement in a quiet suburb. Two officers were wounded in the chase.

A search of the scene of the shooting uncovered a number of pipe bombs laid by the suspects. The bombs were poorly constructed and did not activate. They were probably left to target law enforcement.

Consider the implications of this shooting. While it was marked as a terrorist attack, there was no demonstrable connection to any terror organization. The killers used readily available armaments to take life. Firearms are easy to buy, and easy to use. The abortive attempt to create explosives failed. Explosives are dangerous and difficult to construct, difficult to carry, and difficult to conceal.

The three and a half minutes that it took law enforcement to respond enabled the killers to complete their attack, just as has happened with other incidents. While three minutes is a decent response time, it was essentially worthless to the victims. Additional time was wasted looking for the killers instead of aiding the victims. This is understandable, but it is quite possible that more lives might have been saved had law enforcement aided the victims.

It took law enforcement from 11:00 a.m. to after 3 p.m. to find and kill the perpetrators. At least 300 officers and agents from various city, state and federal agencies were involved in the event, which also included a surveillance aircraft and various military-style armored vehicles like the Bearcat.

Some law enforcement officials claimed that this kind of attack demonstrates the need for police to acquire such equipment. Yet, the armored vehicles did not prevent the attack. By this logic, in order to ensure that some people are able to own firearms, we must create a military-state in order to be safe from armed assailants. That military state will be used against civilians; it is only a matter of time. In the absence of firearms, there would be no need for such drastic action.

The cost of the operation must include all law enforcement officers, their time, vehicles, and ammunition, damage to buildings and the enormous cost incurred by the victims. Should victims and taxpayers be forced to pay the costs incurred in these events, just to protect the right of gun owners to own firearms?

The arms industry makes attacks like this possible by selling such things as tactical gear and load bearing vests. The firearms are easier to carry and fire, and extra ammunition is readily available on the vests. We should not make this kind of attack easier to carry out. There is no need for civilians to own gear like this, or increasingly lethal firearms.

We waste time blaming terrorism for the attack, rather than targeting the firearms that made the attack possible. The motives for these massacres are ultimately irrelevant. Knowing the motive is unlikely to prevent an attack. Instead of targeting the motive for the attack, we should remove the ability to attack with such lethal force. That is what firearms provide.

The World Methodist Council urged prayer and support for the victims and for those affected by this crime motivated by hate. What they neglected to do was to fight for more stringent gun laws. That will go a long way towards ensuring that massacres do not happen.

The United Methodist Church urged members to *"work to end racism and hatred, to seek peace with justice and to live the prayer that the Lord gave -us.."* While ending hatred is fine, it is highly unlikely to happen. Ending gun violence, however, is something that we can do together.

The New York Times published a front-page editorial, the first in 95 years. It wrote,

> "It is a moral outrage and a national disgrace that civilians can legally purchase weapons designed specifically to kill people with brutal speed and efficiency"

The publisher wrote that the editorial is, *"to deliver a strong and visible statement of frustration and anguish about our country's inability to come to terms with the scourge of guns."*

President Obama said,

We have a pattern now of mass shootings in this country that has no parallel anywhere else in the world"

He asked for laws to prevent people on the No Fly List from purchasing firearms. While preventing those people from purchasing firearms is a good idea, it will not change the reality of gun violence in the United States. It will not change the massacres. It will also violate civil liberties without due process.

Targeting small slithers of the populations will do nothing to change the reality of gun violence. We need laws to reduce guns in society. The New York Times is correct. Unless and until we can accomplish that, death will continue to plague our society.

It is sad that anti-Muslim hate crimes increased following the massacre. Yet, a Muslim campaign raised money to assist victims' families in the most successful crowd-funding venture ever launched by Muslims.

Republican presidential candidates responded by saying that the United States is at war. Chris Christie claimed that *this a new world war and it won't look like the last two. And this is one where it's radical Islamic jihadists everyday are trying to kill Americans and disrupt and destroy our way of life."*

Donald Trump called for a complete ban on Muslims entering the United States *"until our country's representatives can figure out what's going on"*. His statement was met with widespread condemnation.

The reality is that Americans, not Muslims, carry out the vast majority of gun crimes, deaths and injuries. In point of fact, terrorism is something very remote from the American homeland. It may happen in other countries, but not here. We experience gun crime because of the prevalence of firearms. Politicians should refrain from changing the subject by pointing to symptoms, instead of causes.

Trying to advance an anti-Muslim agenda instead of honestly attacking gun violence is just ideological dishonesty. The fact is, Islam is almost no threat to the American homeland. It may threaten the interests of industries like the oil industry, but there is no reason that we should pay to support the oil industry.

Charleston Church Shooting

On June 17th, 2015, Dylan Roof took the lives of 9 people and injured three others, including the pastor, during a church service. The Emanuel AME Church was famed for organizing during the Civil Rights Era, slavery and Black Lives Matter. This is probably the reason that Roof targeted the church.

Some people have suggested a strong resemblance between this shooting and the bombing of an African American church in Birmingham, Alabama during which the KKK killed four black girls and injured 14 others. This served to spark the 1960s Civil Rights Movement.

Roof was an avowed White Supremacist who wanted to spark a race war. Before the shooting, Roof posted a racist manifesto on-line. He posed for pictures surrounded by emblems associated with white supremacy. This included the Confederate battle flag and the flags of apartheid South Africa and Rhodesia (now Zimbabwe). Following the shooting, the South Carolina legislature voted to remove the flag from the State Capitol. This was the largest mass shooting at a place of worship since 1991[34].

The killer used a Glock handgun and carried eight magazines holding hollow-point bullets[35]. During the attack, a young man asked him why he was attacking churchgoers. He replied, *"I have to do it. You rape our women and you're taking over our country.*

And you have to go." He is also reported as saying, *"You want something to pray about? I'll give you something to pray about."*[36]

Roof planned the attack for six months, targeting the Emanuel AME Church because of its role in African American history. Another of his proposed targets was the College of Charleston. He told friends of his plans, but he was not taken seriously. He set up a website that was an online manifesto containing his opinions of Blacks, Jews, Hispanics and East Asians.

His motivation was the killing of Trayvon Martin, which he read about online. He decided that George Zimmerman had been in the right, and he was unable to understand why the case became notorious. He discovered the website of the Council of Conservative Citizens where he came across cases of whites killed by African Americans. This probably further radicalized him.

Roof had a prior narcotics conviction that should have prevented him from obtaining a firearm. An error within the background check system kept the conviction from appearing on his record. This allowed him to purchase his firearm.

The reaction from President Obama,

"I've had to make statements like this too many times. Communities have had to endure tragedies like this too many times. Once again, innocent people were killed in part because someone who wanted to inflict harm had no trouble getting their hands on a gun…We as a country will have to reckon with the fact that this type of mass violence does not happen in other advanced countries."[37]

The background check system clearly failed to prevent Roof from obtaining a firearm. That is not because the system does not work, or that it is not worth having. The system needs improvement. The background check system ought to be used to prevent violent people from obtaining firearms.

President Obama had to face the nation far too often with gun massacres. Yet, Congress was incapable of taking concerted action to change that dynamic. We cannot put guards in every public space to prevent violence. The costs are exorbitant, and create an increasingly militaristic society.

I found many of the reactions disappointing. The religious community for the most part issued statements echoing thoughts and prayers. While I understand the religious need for thoughts and prayers, it is only when we take concrete action to change that things will change.

The Council of Bishops of the United Methodist Church issued a statement that was almost a duplicate of the statement issued after the church shooting in Sutherland springs. It spoke more about God's kingdom than about the victims.

The Christian Methodist Episcopal Church asked people to join in prayer for the healing of the families, The World Council of Churches offered prayers for healing to the wounded and traumatized.

The churches took this as an opportunity to preach rather than to take concerted action to end gun violence. If the churches condemned the culture of gun ownership, we might have concerted action. If the churches, mosques, and tabernacles withdrew their support for members of Congress who refuse to take action to restrict firearms, we may have fewer deaths.

Republicans in Congress refused to acknowledge the central issue, which was access to guns, preferring to misdirect the conversation with talk of mental illness. They also claimed that it was a tragic, but random act. It took some time for most Republican candidates to accept that the event was motivated by racism.

Jon Stewart, host of the Daily Show issued a monologue on his show in words to this effect: "In response to Islamic terrorism, politicians declare that they will do whatever it takes to keep America safe, often justifying torture. Yet, they respond to mass shootings as, *"crazy is as crazy does"*.[38] There is clearly an acceptance among politicians of race violence, but not of Islamic violence."

The Council of Conservative Citizens, condemned the attack, but claimed that Roof had some legitimate grievances. Issuing a statement like that in the wake of a massacre is just a roundabout way of justifying the act[39]. The Council is a white nationalist group tied to many Republican politicians in the American South. Among its principles is opposition to the mixing of the races.

A lawyer for the NRA placed the blame on the pastor for not allowing concealed weapons in the church[40]. The pastor who was a state representative voted against legislation allowing concealed handguns in public places. Ultimately, it is the NRA's obsession with guns everywhere that leads directly to massacres. The NRA misdirects attention from its policy of arming everyone by continuing to blame anything not related to firearms.

This attack allowed a white supremacist to take the lives of churchgoers with firearms readily available to every American citizen. It is one more demonstration that the ready availability of firearms in society leads to more death than would otherwise be the case.

Binghamton Shootings

Jiverly Antares Wong, an ethnic Chinese born in Vietnam, carried out the shootings at the American Civic Association immigration center in Binghamton, New York. He killed 13 people and injured four others before taking his own life. The motive for the massacre appears to have been anger at his own inability to comprehend English, which left him with feelings of being "degraded and disrespected"[41].

Once again, there appears to be little evidence that he was mentally ill, rather he was angry at his lack of verbal skill, which he expressed on the object of his anger, the center in which he was ostensibly learning English. His anger may also have been fomented by his dismissal from a vacuum cleaner factory and his inability to procure employment.

The reaction to the shootings was predictable. President Obama referred to the killings as senseless violence, offering sympathy and prayers for the victims, while the governor of New York ordered state flags flown at half-staff. The perpetrators' parents apologized for their sons' actions. The president, speaking in Mexico also said that we "need to deal with assault weapons that...are helping to fuel extraordinary violence.[42]" The possibilities of gun restrictions were not considered. None of these actions will mitigate further gun violence, or prevent future attacks, but comprehensive gun regulation just might.

Chuck Schumer and Kirsten Gillibrand, both senators in New York sponsored a ban on LCM's, which predictably did not pass the Senate. The gun lobby, as predictably claimed that there is "no correlation between the size or arbitrary capacity of a detachable magazine and violent crime[43]". If the latter were true, the gun lobby would have no problem banning large capacity magazines, since there would be no practical reason to use them. LCM's are used because the shooter has no reason to reload until the magazine is empty, making large-scale shootings easier. The only feasible reason for an LCM is a massacre.

One of the survivors, a receptionist who was critically injured has asked for a federal ban on LCM's. Wong fired 97 bullets in less than two minutes with a 9mm Beretta and .45 Beretta. He used 30 bullet magazines during the shooting. The receptionist must now live with the horror of what happened to her, knowing that an ineffectual Congress, and the President, are unlikely to do anything to alleviate gun violence.

Naval Sea Systems Command

The most recent massacre in the U.S. happened at a navy yard in Washington D.C. The gunman, Aaron Alexis killed 12 people and injured eight others, armed with a shotgun. He killed a security guard and took his 9mm semi-automatic pistol to use during his rampage. Taking a position on a fourth floor walkway, he fired down into a lobby from which people were entering a first floor cafeteria. It took several law enforcement agencies thirty minutes to neutralize the gunman, which brings into question the idea that armed civilians would have been able to stop the gunman as the gun lobby often claims. Trained officers were unable to subdue the killer, who was still able to kill with impunity, including wounding an officer.

The killer was cited on eight separate occasions for misconduct, as well as for discharging a weapon within the limits of Fort Worth, Texas. A neighbor in that incident said that he had fired shots up into her apartment, which she believed was "done intentionally". She claimed that he often angrily confronted her about making too much noise and that he frightened her[44]. He was also arrested in Seattle for shooting out the tires on a vehicle, in what he described as an anger-fueled blackout.

The standard claim, as with other mass shootings was that Alexis was mentally ill, citing instances of paranoia, auditory hallucination, and a sleep disorder. Many people exhibit various symptoms of paranoia, such as anxiety, fear or delusion, including members of Congress and many political groups like the Tea Party and the NRA. Paranoia is a controversial diagnosis that may manifest in a multitude of disorders, from depression to schizophrenia without any firm features or classification[45]. Equally, sleep disorders are common within society, and have little connection with violence. Up to 70% of Americans experience some form of sleep disorder, and most are not violent. Individuals may also hear voices without suffering from diagnosable mental illness[46].

The Veterans Administration had reportedly treated Alexis for mental illness, and despite this, he was not declared unfit for duty. Further reporting claimed that the VA treated him for his sleep disorder, not mental illness. We have little idea how serious his purported psychological problems were. Pundits continue to blame mental illness, rather than the more credible anger management issues displayed by the killer, and despite the paucity of evidence connecting any alleged mental illness with violence. The remaining question is why he was allowed to purchase a firearm, despite his history of misconduct and weapons charges. His ability to procure a firearm was far more predictive of a future massacre than his purported and poorly reported mental illness.

In a scene reminiscent of every other massacre in President Obama's two terms, the President pledged to ensure that the perpetrators would be held responsible. Predictably, flags were lowered to half-staff, while the Defense Secretary, Chuck Hagel laid a wreath at the Navy Memorial plaza. The President also stated that we have to have another look at gun restrictions. Congress, like the gun lobby, will wait for the furor, what there is of it, to die down, and quietly shelve any substantive changes to gun policy.

Even the President insists that we should keep guns from the mentally ill, continuing attempts to target the wrong group of people. People as a group, all people, cannot be trusted with firearms, and until that reality is acknowledged, this nation will continue to bury innocent people, allowing the neuroses and paranoia of the gun brigade to rule the debate.

Instead of tackling gun regulation, much of the debate centered around security at U.S. military facilities, which was reminiscent of the NRA demanding law enforcement officers at every school after the Newtown shootings. It makes one wonder when legislators will realize that too many guns result in gun violence and massacres, not the lack of armed guards at military installations. The perpetrator in this instance shot the security guard and took his weapon, which is as likely as what might happen at a school or any other facility. Pundits and officials drew the incorrect conclusions from this massacre, as they have other tragedies, focusing on security and mental illness rather than on the free availability of firearms and on anger management, stress or other precipitating events.

Wayne LaPierre speaking after the shootings demanded "more armed security on military bases", or what he termed "layers of security around our military bases." Considering the extremely low probability of a massacre like this on military bases, LaPierre suggests spending billions of dollars to fuel his neuroses and create an environment of paranoia, using funds that would be better spent on the country's crumbling infrastructure. By far the cheapest option is to remove the threat of guns by removing the guns; that would be cheaper, safer and more effective.

LaPierre continued,

> "We need to look at letting the men and women that know firearms and are trained in them do what they do best, which is protect and survive."

Consider the implications of arming every service member on a base. When one of those members goes on a rampage, the rest of the people on the base cannot be certain who the enemy is. Since everyone is armed, anyone with a weapon will be considered suspect. The instant one responder sees someone with a gun he is likely to return fire, but what if the target is not the shooter. Now you have two people shooting at one another, followed by other armed personnel, which quickly escalates as people begin firing at one another, not knowing who the original shooter is. The result is panic, pandemonium and disaster. The presence of firearms does not solve the problem; they only make the situation worse, as they do in all American life.

LaPierre, as usual is living in John Wayne's world, where people square up in the town center and draw their firearms on command. He clearly does not understand live fire situations, in which the script is not carefully written beforehand. He again brought up the mental health system, without proposing anything substantive and reasonable. Consider the cost of testing every person in the country for mental health issues, as opposed to destroying the firearms. LaPierre demonstrated his authoritarian ambitions by saying,

> "Indict violent criminals. Get them off the street. Indict people that are having mental health problems; get them into treatment. Enforce the federal gun laws…Fix the mental health system and lets get our fiscal house into order so that we can stop releasing the bad guys onto the street."

There is so much that is wrong with this statement that it would take another book this size to cover all that turf. The U.S. indicts more people and has more people in prison than any other nation on Earth. People still commit violent crimes. Clearly, mass incarceration does not work. Indicting people with mental health problems would involve locking up a good 20% of the population.

The gun lobby is not prepared to pay for all this. Fixing the mental health system would be wonderful, if we could just allow Obamacare to enter the mainstream and extend the mental health system to the entire population. Prisons release people when their sentence has been served or they are deemed safe to release. Keeping them incarcerated costs money, while conservatives are manically cutting budgets. Destroying the guns is far cheaper and more effective.

What is startling is that despite the death toll, most coverage of this massacre by all media stopped after less than a week. It is as though the lives lost were of little consequence, and that the People have far better things to do than be concerned about our incessant death toll by firearm. The gun massacres experienced by the American people have become acceptable, prosaic, and expected as the price to be paid for our putative Second Amendment rights. Coverage on NPR again showed the gun lobby's complete disregard of their moral responsibility for gun violence[47].

What is even more disconcerting is that each time there is a massacre, the media immediately ask the NRA, through Wayne LaPierre, and Gun Owners of America and other gun proponents for their comment, but seldom those who advocate gun restrictions. The conversation becomes one-sided, with people only exposed to pro-gun advocacy, and never hearing the gun control arguments. This smacks of an ethical bankruptcy and the imposition of pro-gun ideology, which perpetuates gun violence.

Aurora, Colorado

The killing in Aurora, Colorado, of over 12 people in a movie theater, did little to motivate lawmakers to introduce gun restrictions around the nation. There was a little public outrage, which died down quickly. Neither presidential candidate Barack

Obama nor Mitt Romney had much to say about gun regulation, at a time when guns are killing more than thirty thousand people each year.

James E. Holmes, dressed in protective clothing including ballistic helmet, bullet resistant leggings, throat protector, groin protector and tactical gloves, set off gas canisters and opened fire in the theater with a 12 gauge Remington shotgun and a S&W semi-automatic rifle with 100-round magazine. He also used a Glock 22 when the S&W jammed after firing 45 bullets. He killed 12 people and injured 70. Surprisingly few lawmakers, including Democrats spoke out against the violence. As with other mass shooters, Holmes had stockpiled thousands of rounds of ammunition.

The pro-gun lobby claimed after the Aurora shooting that if more people had been armed in the Aurora Theater, the killer might not have killed as many people. If every person in that theater had been armed, the result would have been vastly more horrific. It is almost impossible, in many shooting situations to determine who the original shooter is, where he or she might be standing or sitting, and whether it is safe to neutralize that person.

A theater is a dark, smoky room, in which it is difficult to make out someone sitting two seats down. If everyone had been armed, someone may have neutralized the shooter, but who is to say that others would not have mistaken the new shooter for the original shooter. The result would quite probably have been complete mayhem, with people shooting wildly in all directions. A great many more people may well have been killed or injured.

In battlefield conditions, it is difficult to make out which side people are on, which is why the rules of war dictate the wearing of uniforms. Even that does not guarantee that friendly fire incidents do not happen, and they most definitely do; and that is among people trained for battlefield conditions. The shooter in Aurora was not wearing a uniform, and it would have been difficult or impossible to know where the shots were coming from. Arming the entire theater is an absurd idea that was not clearly thought out.

The NRA response was, as it usually is, "Our thoughts and prayers are with the victims, their families and the community. The NRA will not have any further comment until all the facts are known[48]". There was no further response, which is the way the NRA prefer it. The group does not want to get its hands dirty, or to make itself a target, so to speak. They know that the fury of the people will subside and they can continue on their merry way, promoting products that kill, just as the tobacco industry used to do and still does. The facts of the situation were not complex, or difficult to understand. A young male used his semi-automatic weapons and large capacity magazines to kill people in a theater.

The political response was equally foreseeable. A candlelight vigil was held the evening after the shooting. The President ordered flags flown at half-mast. The campaigns of President Obama and Mitt Romney suspended advertising in Colorado. The President gave a nationally televised speech. World leaders sent condolences. Two bills circulated in Congress to ban LCM's such as the 100-round drum magazine, the passage of which was highly unlikely according to Carolyn McCarthy (D-NY) sponsor of the House bill[49]. The President stated that he wanted to

> "Work with existing laws rather than new ones to keep weapons from dangerous individuals".

John Boehner, House leader said[50],

> "The President has made clear that he is not going to use this horrific event to push for new gun laws. I agree".

The President expressed shock and sadness, saying that his administration would support the people of Aurora. Mitt Romney expressed deep sadness and prayer. Dozens of politicians produced statements that could have been drawn from the same playbook, sadness, prayers and heartbreak. Not a single politician said that they would move heaven and earth to introduce substantive gun restrictions. Their prayers, offered in every tragedy, have not changed a single thing, or saved a single life. The country does not need prayers; it needs someone, anyone, with courage to stand up to gun industry bullies and thugs. There are clearly no George Washington's or Franklin Roosevelt's here.

Yet again, nothing was done to mitigate gun violence. After the weeping, wailing, and gnashing of teeth, Congress and the President exhibited their traditional terror of the gun lobby and did nothing substantive. As a result, more people will die, gun violence will continue unabated, and at some point, we will have another massacre, at which time we will start the weeping and wailing once more, to no avail.

In a webcast following the disaster, the NRA glossed over the shooting, spending most of its time pulverizing the United Nations for having the temerity to try and curb global firearm sales. The lack of empathy for the victims is a defining feature of the gun lobby response to every instance of gun violence, especially massacres. Their sole responsibility is to increase gun sales in the United States and around the world, regardless of the harm done to gun shot victims. As with other cases, they refuse to comment until "all the facts are known"; in other words, ignore the disaster until everyone has forgotten what happened. The highly probable link between gun violence in this country and the ready availability of small arms cannot stop their gun sales[51].

The NRA response to the shootings was to solicit more funds from their members,

> "The future of your Second Amendment Rights will be at stake. And nothing less than the future of our country and our freedom will be at stake"[52]

Instead of waiting for a decent period, the NRA used the massacre to enrich itself and ensure more funding for lobbying activities. That in turn ensures more legislators voting against gun reform and introducing relaxed gun legislation in state houses. In riposte to the NRA statement, the fact is that the freedom of people who do not possess or want to possess firearms is at stake. We have our freedoms ripped away by gun proponents, who force extreme firearms on our society, making us all less safe. The palpable threat to a peaceful society posed by people possessing extreme firearms places that free society at great risk of instability.

Gun sales in Colorado spiked after the massacre, with applications for background checks rising 43%[53]. The ensuing gun debate revolved around the ease of access that Holmes had to semi-automatic rifles and LCM's. As with every other massacre, nothing was done, no gun limitation legislation, no bans on semi-automatic weapons, especially assault weapons, and no bans on ammunition purchases or LCM's.

Sikh Temple, Wisconsin

Wade Michael Page, the killer of six people at a Sikh temple in Wisconsin was a white supremacist that had spoken before of an impending holy war[54]. He purchased his weapons openly, passed background checks and paid cash for his firearms along with three 19-round magazines. What his killings demonstrate is the ease with which militia groups or other groups whose philosophy is based on hatred of others, can obtain and use inordinate firepower against unsuspecting and vulnerable civilians.

The growing number of militia groups arming themselves for a war against government, or to take back the country, often in the name of disaffected white men, is an ominous threat to the stability and security of the nation. The risk of insurrection, even if unsuccessful grows exponentially along with the killing power of firearms, insufficient regulation, excessive quantities of ammunition and the push for concealed carry and Stand Your Ground laws. Ordinary civilians having no need for extreme weapons are powerless against radical and fanatical groups or individuals, as Southern, Midwestern and Mountain West legislatures remove whatever regulation is available to protect people.

The reaction to the killing was, like other massacres, predictable; President Obama offered condolences; flags flew at half-staff; the President called for soul searching; the governor issued sympathies and he U.S. ambassador to India attended prayers for the victims. The only concrete action, other than futile protests against the U.S. government in India, was a Congressional hearing on hate-crimes before a Senate sub-committee. No restrictions on firearms, monitoring of hate groups, or any other concrete legislation was offered. The victims today are forgotten, except perhaps within the Sikh community.

Tucson, Arizona

After the killing of six people, including nine-year-old Christina Taylor-Green and the shooting of Rep. Gabrielle Giffords, Gov. Jan Brewer, Senate President Russell Pearce and House Speaker Kirk Adams all said that they would not pursue new limits on guns or ammunition[55]. A bill allowing guns on college campuses and universities was to be tabled instead.

Blame for the shooting flew with intensity; some blamed partisan political bickering; others blamed Loughner's diagnosis of paranoid schizophrenia; Sarah Palin was blamed for gun-laced speeches and her website which irresponsibly displayed a map with Gifford's district marked by crosshairs. Some claimed that Jared Loughner, the perpetrator, was an anarchist who hated all politicians.

The reaction was comparable to other tragedies; anti-gun-violence activists wanted restrictions on firearms, ammunition, and high capacity magazines, especially since Loughner was stopped from continuing his rampage when he ran out of ammunition. President Obama led a nationally televised memorial service. Both political parties called for a cooling of political rhetoric, and bipartisanship. Sarah Palin lambasted her critics by saying that her map did not cause the massacre, accusing the press of a 'blood libel' for blaming her and the right wing. Tucson Tea Party member Trent Humphries proposed that gun restrictions not be discussed until all those killed were buried.

The sheriff of Pima County,

> When you look at unbalanced people, how they respond to the vitriol that comes out of certain mouths about tearing down the government. The anger, the hatred, the bigotry that goes on in this country is getting to be outrageous.... We have become the Mecca for prejudice and bigotry"

The combination of malicious political partisanship, mostly on the far right, and access to extreme firearms will undoubtedly have an impact on many people. Some of those people will arm themselves with multiple extreme firearms and ammunition and ready themselves for the day on which they will either defend against government, or attack vulnerable targets or their government. Some states go so far as to make it illegal for federal agents to carry out their duties in those states, threatening them with arrest and imprisonment. Whether that is the case with this perpetrator remains to be seen, as the killer ironically invoked his Fifth Amendment rights after exercising his Second.

It is in Arizona, a crucible of intolerance, that Loughner chose to massacre his victims, just as it is the Southern, Mid-Western and Mountain West states that see high rates of gun violence. Arizona insists on encouraging people to possess firearms, including concealed carry laws that do not require a permit and allows weapons in bars, a particularly deadly combination. In few other states are firearms and liquor allowed to mix without hindrance. It will not be too long before there is a deadly massacre in a bar or restaurant where weapons are allowed.

Comment was received from various quarters including British Prime Minister, David Cameron, Spanish Prime Minister Jose Luis Rodriguez Zapatero and Cuba's Fidel Castro. Sen. Chuck Schumer called for a, examination of gun regulations in the U.S. including prohibiting high capacity magazines (HCM's) and prohibiting those rejected for military service because of drug use. Homeland Security Committee chairman introduced a bill banning firearms within 1,000 feet of federal buildings. Rep. Caroline McCarthy introduced legislation to ban sales of HCM's. None of this proposed legislation became law. For some bizarre reason, the Westboro Baptist Church announced the picketing of the funeral for shooting victim Christine Taylor-Green.

Like other mass shootings, bombastic rhetoric was the order of the day, mostly filled with sound and fury, and very little of practical value. The calls for limits on firearms or magazines came to naught. Politicians, the media and the public returned to the safety of their feathered beds, secure in the knowledge that they had strutted, fretted and banged the gavel. Ultimately, the shooting of a member of Congress had as much effect on that Congress as a butterfly's flapping wings have on the formation of hurricanes. Perhaps in some future generation, the germination of some gun limitation legislation will send a convulsion through Congress and sanity will prevail. I have my doubts, given the detachment from reality that possesses denizens in this nations' halls of power. Postponing anti-gun-violence legislation ensured, as it was intended, that nothing be done to mitigate massacres.

Conclusion

I have not listed all the massacres that have occurred in the United States. I have listed many that resonated with me, or are indicative of a pattern of destruction.

Every tragedy brings with it an outpouring of grief from many quarters. What is troubling is that the outpouring does not last long. The gun lobby, and by that I mean the NRA and its adherents know full well that they have only to wait long enough and the tragedy will disappear from people's minds. They know that they can then continue to sell death and destruction around the country and around the world.

The United States has become a nation that is not safe for many people. In many sectors of the country gun violence is no longer an epidemic it is endemic. It has become an accepted part of living in America. Gun deaths in New Orleans rank with the most violent nations on Earth.

We cannot continue to accept this as part of living in America, the consequence of a poorly worded Constitutional Amendment. We have to act judiciously. Today.

Notes

[1] <http://www.sourcewatch.org/index.php/Stand_Your_Ground> The Center for Media and Democracy. Last Accessed October 28th, 2013.

[2] <http://articles.washingtonpost.com/2012-04-07/national/35452643_1_new-law-american-law-justice-system>. Marc Fisher and Dan Eggen. April 7th, 2012. "Stand Your Ground laws coincide with jump in justifiable homicide cases."

[3] <http://www.rawstory.com/rs/2012/04/17/alec-eliminates-task-force-on-social-issues/>. Andrew Jones. April 17th, 2013. "ALEC eliminates task force on social issues."

[4] <http://www.nytimes.com/2005/04/27/national/27shoot.html?_r=0>, New York Times, Abby Goodnough, April 27th, 2005. "Florida expands right to use deadly force in self-defense."

[5] <http://www.nytimes.com/2005/04/27/national/27shoot.html?_r=0>, New York Times, Abby Goodnough, April 27th, 2005. "Florida expands right to use deadly force in self-defense."

[6] <http://www.thenation.com/blog/166978/how-alec-took-floridas-license-kill-law-national#>, John Nichols, The Nation, March 21st 2012. "How ALEC took Florida's 'License to kill' law national."

[7] <http://www.foxnews.com/politics/2013/02/23/task-force-says-tand-your-ground-is-good-law/> AP, February 23rd, 2013. "Task force backs Florida's 'Stand Your Ground' law."

[8] < http://www.childrensdefense.org/child-research-data-publications/data/state-data-repository/cits/2011/children-in-the-states-2011-florida.pdf>. Children's Defense Fund. Last accessed April 23rd, 2014.

[9] States in which a defendant was required to   in 2006 include, (Alabama, Alaska, Arkansas,
Connecticut, Delaware, Florida, Hawaii, Iowa, Maine, Maryland, Massachusetts, Minnesota, Missouri, Nebraska, New Hampshire, New Jersey, New York, North Carolina, Ohio, Pennsylvania, Rhode Island, South Carolina.

[10] <http://en.wikipedia.org/wiki/Self_defense>. Last Accessed July 30th, 2013. "Self Defense: Legal Aspects."

[11] <http://en.wikipedia.org/wiki/Self_defense>. Last Accessed July 30th, 2013. "Self Defense: Legal Aspects.".

[12] <http://en.wikipedia.org/wiki/Self_defense>. Last Accessed July 30th, 2013. "Self Defense: Legal Aspects.".

[13] <http://www.latimes.com/news/nation/nationnow/la-na-nn-george-zimmerman-marissa-alexander-20130717,0,4248003.story>. Benjamin Mueller. July 20th, 2013. "Marissa Alexander case emerges as symbol after Zimmerman verdict."

[14] <http://econweb.tamu.edu/mhoekstra/castle_doctrine.pdf>. Cheng Cheng: Texas A&M University, Department of Economics. Mark Hoekstra: Texas A&M University.

[15] <http://econweb.tamu.edu/mhoekstra/castle_doctrine.pdf>. Cheng Cheng: Texas A&M University, Department of Economics. Mark Hoekstra: Texas A&M University.

[16] <http://legal-dictionary.thefreedictionary.com/Criminal+Law>, "Criminal Law". Last Accessed 27th March 2013.

[17] <http://en.wikipedia.org/wiki/Castle_doctrine>. Last Accessed July 31st, 2013. "Castle Doctrine."

[18] <http://www.thenation.com/blog/166978/how-alec-took-floridas-license-kill-law-national#>, John Nichols, The Nation, March 21st 2012. "Poll shows racial divide on view Trayvon Martin case."

[19] <http://www.tampabay.com/news/courts/criminal/many-killers-who-go-free-with-florida-Stand-Your-Ground-law-have-history/1241378>. Kameel Stanley and Connie

Humburg. July 21st, 2012. "Many killers who go free with Florida Stand Your Ground law have history of violence."

[20] <http://econweb.tamu.edu/mhoekstra/castle_doctrine.pdf>. Cheng Cheng: Texas A&M University, Department of Economics. Mark Hoekstra: Texas A&M University.

[21] Chandler B. McClellan and Professor Erdal Tekin, Georgia State University, 2012. States with Stand-Your-Ground laws include Alabama, Arizona, Florida, Georgia, Indiana, Kansas, Kentucky, Louisiana, Michigan, Mississippi, Montana, New Hampshire, Oklahoma, South Carolina, South Dakota, Tennessee, Texas and West Virginia

[22] <http://www.nber.org/papers/w18187.pdf>. Stand Your Ground Laws, Homicides and Injuries, Chandler B. McClellan and Professor Erdal Tekin, Georgia State University, Working paper 18187, June 2012.

[23] < http://chicagopolicyreview.org/2013/02/20/a-license-to-kill/ >. "A license to Kill? Quanic Fullard, Chicago Policy Review, Feb 20th, 2013.

[24] <http://www.huffingtonpost.com/2013/07/21/Stand-Your-Ground-laws_n_3631625.html>. Curt Anderson. July 21st, 2013. "Stand Your Ground laws: despite outcry, repeals unlikely."

[25] <http://www.tampabay.com/news/publicsafety/crime/five-years-since-florida-enacted-Stand-Your-Ground-law-justifiable/1128317> . Ben Montgomery and Colleen Jenkins. October 15th, 2010. "Five years since Florida enacted 'Stand-Your-Ground' law, justifiable homicides are up."

[26] <http://www.tampabay.com/news/publicsafety/crime/five-years-since-florida-enacted-Stand-Your-Ground-law-justifiable/1128317> . Ben Montgomery and Colleen Jenkins. October 15th, 2010. "Five years since Florida enacted 'Stand-Your-Ground' law, justifiable homicides are up".

[27] <http://www.tampabay.com/news/publicsafety/crime/florida-Stand-Your-Ground-law-yields-some-shocking-outcomes-depending-on/1233133>, Kris Hundley, Susan Taylor Martin, Connie Humburg, June 1st, 2012.

[28] <http://www.palmbeachpost.com/news/news/national-govt-politics/Stand-Your-Ground-self-defense-raises-more-questio/nScfb/>. John Lantigua and Niels Heimeriks, October 14th, 2012, Palm Beach Post

[29] <http://www.tampabay.com/news/publicsafety/crime/florida-Stand-Your-Ground-law-yields-some-shocking-outcomes-depending-on/1233133>, Kris Hundley, Susan Taylor Martin, Connie Humburg, June 1st, 2012.

[30] <http://www.tampabay.com/news/publicsafety/crime/florida-Stand-Your-Ground-law-yields-some-shocking-outcomes-depending-on/1233133>, Kris Hundley, Susan Taylor Martin, Connie Humburg, June 1st, 2012. "Florida 'Stand Your Ground law yields some shocking outcomes depending on how law is applied."

[31] <http://www.tampabay.com/news/courts/criminal/drug-dealer-used-Stand-Your-Ground-to-avoid-charges-in-two-killings/1235650>. Kris Hundley. June 16th, 2012. "Drug dealer used Stand Your Ground to avoid charges in two killings."

[32] <http://www.tampabay.com/news/publicsafety/crime/florida-Stand-Your-Ground-law-yields-some-shocking-outcomes-depending-on/1233133>, Kris Hundley, Susan Taylor Martin, Connie Humburg, June 1st, 2012.

[33] <http://www.tampabay.com/news/courts/criminal/many-killers-who-go-free-with-florida-Stand-Your-Ground-law-have-history/1241378>. Kameel Stanley and Connie Humburg. July 21st, 2012. "Many killers who go free with Florida Stand Your Ground law have history of violence."

[34] <http://www.cbsnews.com/8301-504083_162-57594207-504083/darius-simmons-murder-john-henry-spooner-wis-man-76-guilty-in-fatal-shooting-of-13-year-old-teen-

neighbor/>. Crimesider Staff. July 17th, 2013. "Darius Simmons murder: John Henry Spooner, Wis. man, 76, guilty in fatal shooting of 13-year-old teen neighbor."
[35] http://www.tampabay.com/Stand-Your-Ground-law/cases/case_104 Tampa Bay Times.
[36] http://www.tampabay.com/Stand-Your-Ground-law/cases/case_4 Tampa Bay Times.
[37] http://www.tampabay.com/Stand-Your-Ground-law/cases/case_115 Tampa Bay Times, July 16th 2009.
[38] <http://www.tampabay.com/news/publicsafety/crime/florida-Stand-Your-Ground-law-yields-some-shocking-outcomes-depending-on/1233133>, Kris Hundley, Susan Taylor Martin, Connie Humburg, June 1st, 2012. "Florida 'Stand Your Ground law yields some shocking outcomes depending on how law is applied."+
[39] <http://thinkprogress.org/justice/2012/04/10/460965/zimmerman-shoot-kill-troops-military/> Jon Soltz, member of www.VoteVets.org , April 10th, 2012. "George Zimmerman had more legal authority to shoot and kill than our troops do at war."
[40] <http://www.tampabay.com/news/publicsafety/crime/florida-Stand-Your-Ground-law-yields-some-shocking-outcomes-depending-on/1233133>, Kris Hundley, Susan Taylor Martin, Connie Humburg, June 1st, 2012. "Florida 'Stand Your Ground law yields some shocking outcomes depending on how law is applied."
[41] <http://www.washingtonpost.com/national/Stand-Your-Ground-laws-coincide-with-jump-in-justifiable-homicide-cases/2012/04/07/gIQAS2v51S_print.html>. Marc Fisher, Dan Eggen. April 7th, 2012. "Stand Your Ground laws coincide with jump in justifiable-homicide cases."
[42] <http://thinkprogress.org/justice/2012/11/15/1193031/disregarding-empirical-research-florida-panel-largely-endorses-Stand-Your-Ground-law/>. Nicole Flatow. November 15th, 2012. "Disregarding empirical research Florida panel largely endorses Stand Your Ground law."
[43] <http://www.huffingtonpost.com/david-hemenway-phd/Stand-Your-Ground_b_2119322.html>, David Hemenway, Ph. D, Director, Harvard Injury Control Research Center, November 11th, 2012. "Don't ignore the evidence: Stand Your Ground is bad for Florida."
[44] <http://www.tampabay.com/news/publicsafety/crime/florida-Stand-Your-Ground-law-yields-some-shocking-outcomes-depending-on/1233133>, Kris Hundley, Susan Taylor Martin, Connie Humburg, June 1st, 2012. "Florida 'Stand Your Ground law yields some shocking outcomes depending on how law is applied."
[45] http://thinkprogress.org/justice/2012/04/20/468444/half-the-lawmakers-on-florida-Stand-Your-Ground-task-force-are-alec-members-all-supported-Stand-Your-Ground/ , Adam Peck, Apr 20th, 2012. " Half the lawmakers on Florida 'Stand Your Ground' task force are ALEC members, all supported Stand Your Ground."
[46] <http://www.huffingtonpost.com/2013/01/16/Stand-Your-Ground-florida-sybrina-fulton_n_2490026.html>. January 16th, 2013. "Stand Your Ground: Florida Democrats join Sybrina Fulton in fight to repeal law."
[1] Press release by the Brady Center to Prevent Gun Violence.
[2] <http://usatoday30.usatoday.com/news/nation/story/2012-06-09/trayvon-martin-Stand-Your-Ground/55480352/1>, Yamiche Alcindor, USAToday, July 9th, 2012. "Florida expands right to use deadly force in self-defense."
[3] <http://www.flgov.com/wp-content/uploads/2013/02/Citizen-Safety-and-Protection-Task-Force-Report-FINAL.pdf>. "Report of the governors task force on citizen safety and protection." Lt. Gov Jennifer Carroll et al. February 21st, 2013.
[4] <http://usatoday30.usatoday.com/news/nation/story/2012-04-05/trayvon-martin-

poll/54047512/1> Yamiche Alcindor, USAToday, April 6th, 2012.
5 <http://www.youtube.com/watch?v=emias0ESFl0&feature=youtu.be>.
Rightwingwatch.org. Last accessed August 1st, 2013. "Robertson: Zimerman right to
follow Travon Martin for wearing.."
6 <http://www.washingtonpost.com/blogs/post-partisan/wp/2013/02/05/the-rabid-hate-
aimed-at-trayvon-martin/> Jonathon Capehart, February 5th, 2013. "The rabid hate
aimed at Trayvon Martin."
7 <http://mediamatters.org/blog/2012/03/21/the-blaze-do-we-know-trayvon-martin-
wasnt-an-ar/186523> Simon Maloy, March 21st, 2012. "The Blaze: Do we know
Trayvon Mrtin wasn't an arsonist kidnapper."
8 <http://usatoday30.usatoday.com/news/nation/story/2012-06-09/trayvon-martin-
Stand-Your-Ground/55480352/1>, Yamiche Alcindor, USAToday, July 9th, 2012.
"Officials plan to take close look at Stand-Your-Ground laws."
9 <http://www.prwatch.org/news/2012/05/11509/virginia-firm-sells-gun-targets-
resembling-trayvon-martin>, Sara Jerving, May 14th, 2012. "Virginia firm sells gun
argets resembling Trayvon Martin."
10 <http://www.clickorlando.com/news/news/Trayvon-Martin-gun-range-targets-sold-
online/-/9533136/13069306/-/10ffct0z/-/index.html>, Mike DeForest, May 11th, 2012.
11 <http://www.motherjones.com/mojo/2012/05/trayvon-martin-target-practice>. Mark
Follman. May 11th, 2012. "Selling Trayvon Martin for target practice."
1 <http://www.nytimes.com/2013/08/30/opinion/statehouse-swagger-in-the-gun-
debate.html?ref=opinion> . The Editorial Board, New York Times. August 29th, 2013.
"Statehouse swagger in the gun debate."
2 <http://en.wikipedia.org/wiki/Daingerfield_church_shooting>. Last Accessed August
26th, 2013.
3 <http://en.wikipedia.org/wiki/Knoxville_Unitarian_Universalist_church_shooting>.
Last Accessed August 26th, 2013.
4 <http://www.washingtonpost.com/blogs/worldviews/wp/2012/12/17/iranian-
supreme-leader-ali-khamenei-echoes-mike-huckabee-on-newtown-school-shooting/>.
Max Fisher. December 17th, 2012. "Iranian Supreme leader Ali Khamenei echoes
Mike Huckabee on Newtown school shooting."
5 <http://nces.ed.gov/pubs2012/pesschools10/tables/table_02.asp>, Last Accessed
23rd March 2013. National Center for Education Statistics.
6 <http://www.bls.gov/ooh/protective-service/police-and-detectives.htm>. Bureau of
Labor Statistics, 2010. Last accessed September 1st, 2013.
7 <http://www.nationalmemo.com/what-the-nras-school-shield-would-cost/>. David
Cay Johnston. April 3rd, 2013. "What the NRA's 'School Shield' would cost."
8 <http://www.nationalmemo.com/what-the-nras-school-shield-would-cost/>. David
Cay Johnston. April 3rd, 2013. "What the NRA's 'School Shield' would cost.".
9 <http://www.motherjones.com/politics/2013/01/asa-hutchinson-nra-pinkerton-
securitas-lobbyist>. Tim Murphy. Jan 8th, 2013. "NRA private security advocate
works for private security company."
10 <http://www.nationalmemo.com/what-the-nras-school-shield-would-cost/>. David
Cay Johnston. April 3rd, 2013. "What the NRA's 'School Shield' would cost.".
11 <http://www.dailykos.com/story/2012/12/21/1172856/-If-only-armed-guards-
would-stop-a-school-massacre#>. Daily Kos Staff. December 21st, 2012. "If only
armed guards would stop a school massacre."
12 <http://colorlines.com/archives/2012/12/the_school-to-
prison_pipeline_comes_before_the_senate.html>. Julianne Hing. December 13, 2012.
""The School-to-prison pipeline gets its first ever hearing in the Senate."

[13] <http://www.motherjones.com/mojo/2013/04/asa-hutchinson-cops-schools-criminal-records>. Tim Murphy. April 2nd, 2013. "The NRA unveils its school safety plan: More guns."

[14] <http://www.motherjones.com/mojo/2013/04/asa-hutchinson-cops-schools-criminal-records>. Tim Murphy. April 2nd, 2013. "The NRA unveils its school safety plan: More guns.".

[15] <http://colorlines.com/archives/2012/12/the_school-to-prison_pipeline_comes_before_the_senate.html>. Julianne Hing. December 13, 2012. ""The School-to-prison pipeline gets its first ever hearing in the Senate."

[16]

<http://www.justicepolicy.org/uploads/justicepolicy/documents/educationunderarrest_fullreport.pdf>. Last Accessed September 1st, 2013. "Education under arrest: The case against police in schools."

[17]

<http://www.justicepolicy.org/uploads/justicepolicy/documents/educationunderarrest_fullreport.pdf>. Last Accessed September 1st, 2013. "Education under arrest: The case against police in schools."

[18]

<http://www.justicepolicy.org/uploads/justicepolicy/documents/educationunderarrest_fullreport.pdf>. Last Accessed September 1st, 2013. "Education under arrest: The case against police in schools."

[19] <http://uvamagazine.org/short_course/article/how_safe_are_our_schools/#.Uh-IshvUmIo>. Sierra Bellows. Spring 2008 "How safe are our schools: Professor Dewey Cornell traces the roots of violence."

[20] <http://uvamagazine.org/short_course/article/how_safe_are_our_schools/#.Uh-IshvUmIo>. Sierra Bellows. Spring 2008 "How safe are our schools: Professor Dewey Cornell traces the roots of violence.".

[21] <http://www.cdc.gov/violenceprevention/youthviolence/schoolviolence/savd.html>. Last accessed August 29th, 2013.

[22] <http://www.indiana.edu/~safeschl/facts.html>. "The facts about school violence." Last accessed August 29th, 2013.

[23]

<http://www.nasponline.org/resources/crisis_safety/Youth_Gun_Violence_Fact_Sheet.pdf>. Youth gun violence fact sheet. Centres for Disease Control.

[24]

<http://www.slate.com/articles/news_and_politics/map_of_the_week/2012/12/sandy_hook_a_chart_of_all_196_fatal_school_shootings_since_1980_map.html >. Chris Kirk. Slate Magazine, December 2012

[25]

<http://www.rollcall.com/news/stockman_seeks_repeal_of_gun_free_school_zones_law-220658-1.html?zkPrintable=true>. Lauren Smith. January 9th, 2013. "Stockman seeks repeal of gun-free school zones law."

[26] <http://www.motherjones.com/politics/2012/07/mass-shootings-map>. Mark Follman, Gavin Aronsen, Deanna Pan. February 27th, 2013. "A guide to mass shootings in America."

[27] < http://www.huffingtonpost.com/wendy-fontaine/romney-gun-violence-single-parent_b_1972505.html>. Wendy Fontaine. October 17th, 2012. "Why Mitt can't blame us single parents for gun violence."

[28] <http://www.policymic.com/articles/20868/gun-control-is-not-the-answer-to-prevent-mass-killings-education-is>. Michael Cain. January 2013. "Gun control is not

---

the answer to prevent mass killings, education is."

[29] < http://www.newsmax.com/Newswidget/poll-blame-violence-hollywood/2013/01/18/id/472068>. Jim Meyers. January 25th, 2013. "NBC poll: Public blames parents, Hollywood over guns for violence."

[30] http://www.motherjones.com/mojo/2012/12/national-rifle-association-has-video-game-too . Tim Murphy. December 21st, 2012. "NRA blames violent video games for Newtown, but partnered with company that makes them."

[31] < http://futureofchildren.org/futureofchildren/publications/docs/12_02_01_.pdf >. The future of children Volume 12 - Number 2 Summer/Fall 2002. "Children, youth and gun violence."

[32] <http://www.cdc.gov/violenceprevention/youthviolence/stats_at-a_glance/>. Last Accessed August 27th, 2013.

[33] <http://www.tamiu.edu/~cferguson/CJBGames.pdf>. Christopher Ferguson, Stephanie M. Rueda, Amanda M Cruz. Diana E. Ferguson, Stacey Fritz, Shawn M. Smith. "Violent video games and aggression: Causal relationship of byproduct of family violence and intrinsic violence motivation."

[34] <http://www.tamiu.edu/~cferguson/CJBGames.pdf>. Christopher Ferguson, Stephanie M. Rueda, Amanda M Cruz. Diana E. Ferguson, Stacey Fritz, Shawn M. Smith. "Violent video games and aggression: Causal relationship of byproduct of family violence and intrinsic violence motivation.".

[35] <http://www.tamiu.edu/~cferguson/CJBGames.pdf>. Christopher Ferguson, Stephanie M. Rueda, Amanda M Cruz. Diana E. Ferguson, Stacey Fritz, Shawn M. Smith. "Violent video games and aggression: Causal relationship of byproduct of family violence and intrinsic violence motivation.".

[36] <http://www.webmd.com/parenting/features/toy-guns-do-they-lead-real-life-violence>. Lisa Zamowsky. "Toy guns: do they lead to real life violence?"

[1] http://www.huffingtonpost.com/2012/12/14/victoria-jackson-connecticut-school-shooting_n_2303518.html . December 14th, 2012. "Victoria Jackson's Connecticut school shooting post: Former 'SNL' star's tone deaf comment hours after tragedy."

[2] <http://www.wnd.com/2012/07/our-culture-of-death-and-the-batman-shooting/>. Matt Barber. July 20th, 2012. "Our culture of death and the Batman shooting."

[3] <http://cercor.oxfordjournals.org/content/13/2/115.long>. Last accessed August 21st, 2013.

[4] <http://works.bepress.com/john_donohue/8/>. John Donohue, Yale University and Steven D. Levitt, University of Chicago. "The impact of legalized abortion on crime."

[5] <http://www.frc.org/washingtonupdate/dems-still-gunning-for-second-amendment>. Tony Perkins. Family Research Council. "Dems still gunning for second amendment."

[6] <http://www.nytimes.com/2000/04/09/us/they-threaten-seethe-and-unhinge-then-kill-in-quantity.html?pagewanted=all&src=pm>, April 9th, 2000. Ford Fessenden.

[7] <http://www.ncbi.nlm.nih.gov/pubmed/11104447>. May JP, Hemenway D, Owen R, Pitts K. June 28th, 2000. "When criminals are shot: A survey of Washington, DC, jail detainees."

[8] <http://alecexposed.org/w/images/3/37/7J10-Resolution_On_Firearms_Purchase_Waiting_Periods_Exposed.pdf>, Last Accessed march 22nd, 2013.

[9] <http://nij.gov/topics/crime/gun-violence/working-group/wellford/fvrwg-2010-14.htm>, Last Accessed 22nd March, 2013.

[10] <http://www.businessinsider.com/shooting-gun-laws-2012-12>, December17th, 2012.

[11] <http://www.ncbi.nlm.nih.gov/pubmed/8637171> . Sinauer N, Annest JL, Mercy

JA. National Center for Injry Prevention and Control, National Centers for Disease Control and Prevention, Atlanta, GA. "Unintentional, nonfatal firearm-related injuries. A Preventable health burden." June 1996.

[12] < http://content.healthaffairs.org/content/26/2/575.full>. Makinko, James et al. "Reductions in firearm-related mortality and hospitalizations in Brazil after gun control."

[13] http://www.smallarmssurvey.org/armed-actors/civilians.html . Small Arms Survey 2006.

[14] < http://www.insightcrime.org/news-briefs/gun-ban-bogota-homicide>. " Bogotá homicides reach 27 year low after gun ban." Victoria Rossi. September 12th, 2012.

[15] http://www.motherjones.com/politics/2012/09/mass-shootings-investigation , Mark Follman. December 15th, 2012. "More Guns, More Mass Shootings – Coincidence?"

[16] < https://www.ncjrs.gov/pdffiles/165476.pdf >. Cook PJ, Ludwig J. *Guns in America: National survey on private ownership and use of firearms*. National Institute of Justice, Research in Brief. May 1997.

[17] < http://www.ncbi.nlm.nih.gov/pubmed/15261906 >. Johnson RM, Coyne-Beasley T, Runyan CW. Firearm ownership and storage practices, U.S. households, 1992-2002. *American Journal of Preventive Medicine*, 2004; 27(2):173-82.

[18] < https://www.ncjrs.gov/html/ojjdp/nationalreport99/frontmatter.pdf >. Snyder HN, Sickmund M. *Juvenile offenders and victims: 1999 national report*. Washington DC, 1999: Office of Juvenile Justice and Delinquency Programs.

[19] US Department of Treasury, Bureau of Alcohol, Tobacco, and Firearms. *Crime Gun Trace Reports (2000)*

[20] < http://www.ncbi.nlm.nih.gov/pubmed/15625479 >. Richmond T, Branas C, Cheney R, Schwab C. The case for enhanced data collection of gun type. *J Trauma*2004; 57(6)::1356-1360.

[21] < http://www.ncbi.nlm.nih.gov/pubmed/8411275 >. McGonigal MD, Cole J, Schwab CW, Kauder DR, Rotondo MF, Angood PB. Urban firearm deaths: a five-year perspective. *J Trauma*, 1993; 35:532-7.

[22] < https://www.ncjrs.gov/App/publications/abstract.aspx?ID=169680 >. Wintemute GJ. The relationship between firearm design and firearm violence. Handguns in the 1990s. *JAMA*, 1996; 275(22):1749-53.

[23] < http://www.ncbi.nlm.nih.gov/pubmed/9247210 >. Nance ML, Stafford PW, Schwab CW. Firearm injury among urban youth during the last decade: an escalation in violence. *J Ped Surg*, 1997; 32:949.

[24] < http://www.uphs.upenn.edu/ficap/resourcebook/pdf/monograph.pdf >. Firearm Injury in the U.S. Firearm & Injury Center at Penn.

[25] Data collected by the Injury Prevention Journal, the United Nations Office on Drugs and Crime, the general Social Survey and the U.S. Census bureau. Information obtained from CNN.com. Article by Allison Brennan. July 31st, 2012.

[26] Injury Prevention Journal. Based on 2004 National Firearms Survey.

[27] <http://papers.ssrn.com/sol3/papers.cfm?abstract_id=2131606>. Abhay Aneja, John J. Donahue III, Alexandria Zhang. August 22012. "The impact of Right-To-Carry laws and the NRC report: The latest lessons for the empirical evaluation of law and policy."

[28] <http://www.policyarchive.org/handle/10207/96411>. Matthew Miller, Deborah Azrael, David Hemenway. "Firearm availability and unintentional firearm deaths, suicide and homicide among 5-14 year olds."

[29] <http://islandia.law.yale.edu/ayers/Ayres_Donohue_article.pdf>. Ian Ayres, John J Donohue. April 16th, 2003. "Shooting down the 'More guns less crime' hypothesis."

[30] http://www.scientificamerican.com/article.cfm?id=gun-science-proves-arming-

---

untrained-citizens-bad-idea . Michael Shermer. May 8th, 2013. "The science of guns proves arming untrained citizens is a bad idea." From the book "Reducing gun violence in America: Informing policy with evidence and analysis" by Daniel W. Webster and Jon S. Vernick.

[31] <http://www.motherjones.com/politics/2012/09/mass-shootings-investigation>. Mark Follman. December 15th, 2012. "More guns, more mass shootings - coincidence?"

[32] <http://www.motherjones.com/politics/2012/09/mass-shootings-investigation>, Mark Follman. December 15th, 2012. "More Guns, More Mass Shootings – Coincidence?"

[33] <http://www.smallarmssurvey.org/armed-actors/civilians.html>. Small Arms Survey 2006.

[34] <http://www.smallarmssurvey.org/armed-actors/civilians.html>. Small Arms Survey 2006.. Also see Cook and Ludwig (2004).

[35] <http://www.slate.com/articles/news_and_politics/explainer/2012/12/can_armed_citiz ens_stop_mass_shootings_examples_of_armed_interventions.html> . Forrest Wickman. December 8th, 2012. "Do armed citizens stop mass shootings?"

[36] <http://www.motherjones.com/politics/2012/09/mass-shootings-investigation>. Mark Follman. December 15th, 2012. "More guns, more mass shootings - coincidence?"

[37] <http://www.motherjones.com/politics/2012/12/armed-civilians-do-not-stop-mass-shootings>. Mark Follman. December 19th, 2012. "Do armed civilians stop mass shooters? Actually, no"

[38] <http://www.christianpost.com/news/franklin-graham-opposes-gun-control-blames-entertainment-and-evil-for-violent-attacks-89486/>. Stoyan Zaimov. February 5th, 2013. "Franklin opposes gun control: blames entertainment and evil for violent attacks."

[39] <http://www.christianpost.com/news/franklin-graham-opposes-gun-control-blames-entertainment-and-evil-for-violent-attacks-89486/>. Stoyan Zaimov. February 5th, 2013. "Franklin opposes gun control: blames entertainment and evil for violent attacks.".

[40] <http://en.wikipedia.org/wiki/Sandy_Hook_Elementary_School_shooting>. Last accessed August 28th, 2013.

[41] <http://www.christianpost.com/news/franklin-graham-opposes-gun-control-blames-entertainment-and-evil-for-violent-attacks-89486/>. Stoyan Zaimov. February 5th, 2013. "Franklin opposes gun control: blames entertainment and evil for violent attacks."

[42] <http://www.rawstory.com/rs/2013/08/29/pro-gun-republican-shoots-teacher-with-rubber-bullet-during-live-training-exercise/>. Eric W Dolan. August 29th, 2013. "Pro-gun Republican shoots 'teacher' with rubber bullet during live training exercise."

[43] <http://www.rawstory.com/rs/2013/08/29/pro-gun-republican-shoots-teacher-with-rubber-bullet-during-live-training-exercise/> . Eric W Dolan. August 29th, 2013. "Pro-gun Republican shoots 'teacher' with rubber bullet during live training exercise.".

[44] <http://www.huffingtonpost.com/bob-cesca/good-guys-with-guns-will-_b_2638941.html>. Bob Cesca. February 7th, 2013. "Good guys with guns will not stop gun massacres."

[45] <http://www.huffingtonpost.com/bob-cesca/good-guys-with-guns-will-_b_2638941.html>. Bob Cesca. February 7th, 2013. "Good guys with guns will not stop gun massacres.".

46 <http://www.huffingtonpost.com/2013/05/22/andrea-rebello-death-police-defend-officer_n_3318975.html>. May 21st, 2013. "Andrea Rebello death: police union defends officer who shot, killed Hofstra university student."

47 <http://www.newsmax.com/Newsfront/NRA-LaPierre-Boston-Terrorists/2013/05/04/id/502794>. Todd Beamon. May 4th, 2013. "NRA's laPierre: 'Good guys with guns stopped terrorists with guns.'"

1 <http://www.motherjones.com/politics/2012/07/mass-shootings-map>, Mark Follman, Gavin Aronsen, Deanna Pan. February 27th, 2013.

2 http://www.theatlanticwire.com/politics/2012/12/guns-in-america-statistics/60071/ , Elspeth Reeve, December 17th, 2012. "Some uncomfortable Numbers about Guns in America." The Atlantic Wire.

3 <http://www.motherjones.com/politics/2012/07/mass-shootings-map>, Mark Follman, Gavin Aronsen, Deanna Pan. February 27th, 2013.

4 <http://www.washingtonpost.com/blogs/wonkblog/wp/2012/12/14/why-are-mass-shootings-becoming-more-frequent/>, Brad Plumer, December 14th, 2012. "Why are mass shootings becoming more common.". Washington Post.

5 < http://libcloud.s3.amazonaws.com/9/56/4/1242/1/analysis-of-recent-mass-shootings.pdf >. Last accessed September 13th, 2013.

6 < http://libcloud.s3.amazonaws.com/9/56/4/1242/1/analysis-of-recent-mass-shootings.pdf >. Last accessed September 13th, 2013..

7 < http://libcloud.s3.amazonaws.com/9/56/4/1242/1/analysis-of-recent-mass-shootings.pdf > Last accessed September 13th, 2013..

8 <http://www.nytimes.com/2000/04/09/us/they-threaten-seethe-and-unhinge-then-kill-in-quantity.html?pagewanted=all&src=pm>, April 9th, 2000. Ford Fessenden.

9 http://www.freerepublic.com/focus/f-news/3003324/posts . Charlotte and Harriet Childress. April 1st, 2013. "Mass murder a white male, not mental health, issue." Also, see http://articles.washingtonpost.com/2013-03-29/opinions/38124057_1_white-men-mental-health-issues-mass-shootings . Washington Post Opinions. "White men have much to discuss about mass shootings."

10 http://en.wikipedia.org/wiki/List_of_rampage_killers . Last accessed September 13th, 2013.

11 http://en.wikipedia.org/wiki/Fort_Hood_massacre . Last accessed September 13th, 2013.

12 <http://www.freerepublic.com/focus/f-news/3003324/posts>. Charlotte and Harriet Childress. April 1st, 2013. "Mass murder a white male, not mental health, issue." Also, see <http://articles.washingtonpost.com/2013-03-29/opinions/38124057_1_white-men-mental-health-issues-mass-shootings>. Washington Post Opinions. "White men have much to discuss about mass shootings."

13 <http://www.nationalreview.com/articles/335996/newtown-answers-nro-symposium>. An NRO Symposium. December 19th, 2012. "Newtown answers"

14 <http://www.motherjones.com/politics/2012/09/mass-shootings-investigation>, Mark Follman. December 15th, 2012. "More Guns, More Mass Shootings – Coincidence?"

15 <http://www.nytimes.com/2000/04/09/us/they-threaten-seethe-and-unhinge-then-kill-in-quantity.html?pagewanted=all&src=pm>, April 9th, 2000. Ford Fessenden.

16 <http://www.washingtonpost.com/blogs/wonkblog/wp/2012/12/14/why-are-mass-shootings-becoming-more-frequent/>. Brad Plumer, December 14th, 2012.

17 <http://policeforum.org/library/critical-issues-in-policing-series/Blair-UnitedStatesActiveShooterEventsfrom2000to2010Report-Final.pdf>. J. Pete blair, PhD, M. Hunter Martaindale PhD student. Texas State University. "United States

---

active shooter events from 2000 to 2010: Training and Equipment implications."
[18] <http://www.policymic.com/articles/22774/mass-shootings-are-responsible-for-less-than-100-out-of-12-000-annual-homicides-in-the-us>. Matt MacBradaigh. February 2013. "Mass shootings are responsible for less than 100 out of 12,000 annual homicides in the U.S."
[1] <http://news.yahoo.com/blogs/lookout/adam-lanza-newtown-search-warrants-released-131056789.html>, Jason Sickles and Dylan Stableford. 28th March, 2013. "Adam Lanza Search Warrants released".
[2] <http://www.nydailynews.com/news/national/lupica-lanza-plotted-massacre-years-article-1.1291408>, March 17th, 2013. "Lupica: Morbid find suggests murder-obsessed gunman, Adam Lanza plotted Newtown, Connecticut Sandy Hook massacre for years"
[3] <http://en.wikipedia.org/wiki/Newtown_school_shooting>. Last accessed September 16th, 2013.
[4] <http://edition.cnn.com/2012/12/14/us/connecticut-school-shooting/index.html>. Susan Cadiotti, Sarah Aarthun. December 15th, 2012. "Police: 20 children among 26 victims of Connecticut school shooting."
[5] < http://www.bbc.com/news/technology-41484393 > BBC News. October 3rd, 2017. "Technology giants sorry for false news about Las Vegas Gunman".
[6] < https://www.bloomberg.com/news/articles/2017-10-02/fake-news-fills-information-vacuum-in-wake-of-las-vegas-shooting >. October 2nd, 2017. "Google Displayed Fake News in Wake of Las Vegas Shooting".
[7] < https://www.bloomberg.com/news/articles/2017-10-02/fake-news-fills-information-vacuum-in-wake-of-las-vegas-shooting >. October 2nd, 2017. "Google Displayed Fake News in Wake of Las Vegas Shooting".
[8] <https://www.politico.com/magazine/story/2017/10/02/las-vegas-shooting-fake-news-guns-215670 >. October 2nd, 2017. "Misinformation is the New Normal of Mass Shootings".
[9] https://www.politico.com/story/2017/10/02/las-vegas-isis-shooting-media-243383 >. October 2nd, 2017. "Did some media play into ISIS's hands?"
[10] https://www.cnn.com/2017/11/01/politics/trump-vegas-nyc/index.html.> November 1st, 2017. Chris Cillizza. "The stunning difference between Trump's reaction to the Las Vegas shooting and the NYC attack.
[11] https://www.cbsnews.com/news/proposed-bans-on-bump-stocks-have-stalled-in-congress/. November 6th, 2017. "Proposed bans on bump Stocks have stalled in Congress". Rebecca Shabad, CBS News.
[12] https://homelandprepnews.com/stories/24643-bill-ban-high-capacity-gun-magazines-introduced-senate/ >. October 10th, 2017. Alex Murtha. Homeland Preparedness News. "Bill to ban high-capacity gun magazines introduced in Senate".
[13] https://www.theguardian.com/us-news/2017/oct/26/las-vegas-shooting-conspiracy-theories-social-media . >. 26th October, 2017. Sam Levin. "'I hope someone truly shoots you': online conspiracy theorists harass Vegas Victims.
[14] < https://www.longwarjournal.org/archives/2016/06/orlando-terrorist-swore-allegiance-to-islamic-states-abu-bakr-al-baghdadi.php >. Thomas Joscelyn. June 20th, 2016. "Orlando terrorist swore allegiance to Islamic State's Abu Bakr al Baghdadi"
[15] Ibid.
[16] < http://www.latimes.com/nation/nationnow/la-na-orlando-nightclub-shooting-20160612-snap-story.html >. Joe Mozingo Matt Pierce and Tracy Wilkinson. June 13th, 2016. "'An Act of terror and an act of hate': The aftermath of America's worst mass shooting".

17
<http://www.nola.com/politics/index.ssf/2016/06/orlando_shooting_a_quick_respo.html> The Washington Post. June 21st 2016. "Orlando Shooting: A quick response and then a long wait."
18 <https://www.washingtonpost.com/world/national-security/they-took-too-damn-long-inside-the-police-response-to-the-orlando-shooting/2016/08/01/67a66130-5447-11e6-88eb-7dda4e2f2aec_story.html?utm_term=.5191247772c1 > Adam Goldman and Mark Berman. August 1st, 2016. "'They took too damn long': Inside the police response to the Orlando shooting".
19 http://abcnews.go.com/US/orlando-hospitals-bill-pulse-nightclub-massacre-victims/story?id=41639209 >. David Caplan. August 25th, 2016. "Orlando Hospitals won't bill Pulse Nightclub Massacre Victims".
20 https://www.yahoo.com/gma/orlandos-lgbt-community-expresses-relief-city-wants-buy-165927754--abc-news-topstories.html >. Michael Edison Hayden. November 8th, 2016. "Orlando's LGBT community expresses relief city wants to buy Pulse Nightclub."
21 https://en.wikipedia.org/wiki/List_of_school_massacres_by_death_toll >. Wikipedia. Accessed 7th July, 2018.
22 http://www.sun-sentinel.com/local/broward/parkland/florida-school-shooting/fl-florida-school-shooting-guns-20180215-story.html >. Skyler Swisher and Paula McMahon. February 15th, 2018. "'Nikolas Cruz passed background check, including mental health question, to get AR-15 rifle".
23 https://www.nbcmiami.com/news/local/Petition-JROTC-Cadet-Killed-In-Stoneman-Shooting-Deserves-Full-Honors-Military-Burial-474417123.html >. Selima Hussain. February 18th, 2018. "Petition: JROTC cadet killed in Stoneman shooting deserves full honors military burial."
24
http://www.miamiherald.com/news/local/community/broward/article202164039.html >. David Ovalle and David Smiley. February 26th, 2018. "I'm no coward, says deputy who didn't go inside Parkland school during massacre".
25 <http://www.pewstates.org/projects/stateline/headlines/after-giffords-shooting-no-slowdown-for-gun-rights-85899375344>, John Gramlich. January 21st, 2011. "After Giffords Shooting, no Slowdown for Gun Rights"
26 <http://en.wikipedia.org/wiki/Virginia_Tech_massacre#Government_response>. Last accessed September 14th, 2013.
27 <http://en.wikipedia.org/wiki/Virginia_Tech_massacre#Continuing_response>. Last accessed September 14th, 2013.
28 <http://en.wikipedia.org/wiki/San_Ysidro_McDonald's_massacre>
29 < https://www.cbsnews.com/news/texas-shooting-church-in-sutherland-springs-will-be-demolished-pastor-says/ >. CBS News. November 9th, 2017. CBS/AP
30 < https://www.nytimes.com/2017/11/22/us/pastor-frank-pomeroy-sutherland-springs.html >. New York Times. Serge F. Kovaleski. November 22nd, 2017. "'The Day the Pastor Was Away and Evil Came Barging Into His Church".
31 < https://www.washingtonpost.com/news/the-intersect/wp/2017/11/06/a-fake-shooter-and-false-flag-rumors-at-the-hospital-how-dark-online-hoaxes-came-to-texas/?utm_term=.1940c3de545f >. Washington Post. Avi Selk and May Lee Grant, November 6th 2017. "A fake shooter and false flag rumors at the hospital – how dark online hoaxes came to Texas."
32
33 < http://www.christianitytoday.com/news/2017/september/how-many-churches-in-

america-us-nones-nondenominational.html >. "How many Churches Does America Have? More Than Expected". Rebecca Randall. September 14th, 2017.

[34] < https://www.cnn.com/2015/06/19/us/charleston-church-shooting-suspect/index.html >. "Charleston church shooting: Who is Dylann Roof?" December 16th, 2016. Ray Sanchez and Ed Payne. Retrieved 13th March 2018.

[35] < http://www.latimes.com/nation/la-na-roof-hate-crimes-20150722-story.html >. Timothy M. Phelps. July 22nd, 2015. "Dylann Roof indicted on federal hate-crime charges in Charleston church shootings".

[36] < https://www.washingtonpost.com/politics/south-carolina-governor-urges-death-penalty-charges-in-church-slayings/2015/06/19/3c039722-1678-11e5-9ddc-e3353542100c_story.html?utm_term=.57eb4750a2a1 >. Jeremy Borden, Sari Horwitz andJerry Markon. June 19th, 2015. "From victims' families, forgiveness for accused Charleston gunman Dylann Roof".

[37] < https://www.huffingtonpost.com/entry/barack-obama-charleston-shooting_n_7613074> Ashley Alman. 18th June, 2015. "Obama on Charleston shooting: 'This type of mass violence does not happen In opther dadvanced countries.'"

[38] < https://www.rollingstone.com/tv/news/watch-jon-stewarts-heartbreaking-charleston-shooting-monologue-20150619 >. Daniel Kreps. June 19th, 2015. "Watch Jon Stewart's heartbreaking Charleston shooting monologue".

[39] < https://talkingpointsmemo.com/livewire/ccc-dylann-roof-legitimate-grievances >. Catherine Thompson. June 22nd, 2015. "Group that may hav influenced Charleston killer: He had some 'legitimate grievances".

[40] < https://www.yahoo.com/news/nra-executive-suggests-slain-charleston-pastor-blame-gun-043458974.html >. Lisa Maria Garza. June 20th, 2015. "NRA executive suggests slain Charleston pastor to blame for gun deaths."

[41] <http://en.wikipedia.org/wiki/Binghamton_shootings>. Last accessed September 17th, 2013.

[42] <http://www.huffingtonpost.com/paul-helmke/gun-violence-prevention-a_b_192904.html>. Paul Hemke. April 29th, 2009. "Gun violence prevention and Obama's first 100 days: imcomplete."

[43] http://www.huffingtonpost.com/huff-wires/20110404/us-binghamton-shootings/ . Michael Virtanen. April 4th, 2011. "NY mass shooting survivor wants magazine limits."

[44] <http://www.foxnews.com/us/2013/09/17/active-shooter-at-washington-navy-yard/>. September 17th, 2013. "DC gunman was suffering host of mental issues prior to shooting, report says."

[45] <http://en.wikipedia.org/wiki/Paranoia>. Last accessed September 19th, 2013.

[46] <http://en.wikipedia.org/wiki/Auditory_hallucination>. Last accessed September 19th, 2013.

[47] http://thedianerehmshow.org/shows/2013-09-17/gun-violence-and-debate-over-gun-control-legislation . Hosted by Steve Roberts. September 17th, 2013. "Gun Violence and the debate over gun control legislation."

[48] <http://www.cnn.com/2012/07/20/politics/gun-politics/index.html>, Dana Bash, CNN Senior Congressional Correspondent. July 20th, 2012. "For Democrats, Gun politics are bad politics".

[49] <http://usatoday30.usatoday.com/news/nation/story/2012-07-24/aurora-gun-control-debate/56465980/1>. Rick Jervis, John McAuliff. July 24th, 2012. "Colo. rampage adds fuel to gun-control debate."

[50] <http://usatoday30.usatoday.com/news/nation/story/2012-07-24/aurora-gun-control-

---

debate/56465980/1>. Rick Jervis, John McAuliff. July 24th, 2012. "Colo. rampage adds fuel to gun-control debate.".

[51] <http://www.thedailybeast.com/articles/2012/07/22/the-national-rifle-association-s-bizarre-colorado-response.html>, James Warren. July 22nd, 2012. "The National Rifle Association's bizarre Colorado response".

[52] <http://www.businessweek.com/news/2012-08-07/nra-sought-donations-in-days-after-colorado-shootings>, Bloomberg News. Michael C. Bender. August 7th, 2012. "NRA sought donations after Colorado Shootings.

[53] <http://www.denverpost.com/news/ci_21142159/gun-sales-up-since-tragedy>. Sara Burnett. July 23rd, 2012. "Aurora theater shooting: gun sales up since tragedy."

[54] <http://en.wikipedia.org/wiki/Sikh_temple_mass_killings#Perpetrator. Last accessed September 14th. 2013.

[55] <http://www.pewstates.org/projects/stateline/headlines/colorado-theater-shooting-revives-gun-rights-debate-85899406554>, "Colorado Shooting revives Gun Rights Debate", July 23rd, 2012, Jim Malewitz.